P9-EME-788

FREDERICK DOUGLASS

FREDERICK DOUGLASS

Sharman Apt Russell

Senior Consulting Editor
Nathan Irvin Huggins
Director
W.E.B. Du Bois Institute for Afro-American Research
Harvard University

CHELSEA HOUSE PUBLISHERS
New York   Philadelphia

Editor-in-Chief   Nancy Toff

Executive Editor   Remmel T. Nunn

Managing Editor   Karyn Gullen Browne

Copy Chief   Juliann Barbato

Picture Editor   Adrian G. Allen

Art Director   Giannella Garrett

Manufacturing Manager   Gerald Levine

Staff for FREDERICK DOUGLASS

Senior Editor   Richard Rennert

Associate Editor   Perry King

Editorial Assistant   Laura-Ann Dolce

Copy Editor   Gillian Bucky

Associate Picture Editor   Juliette Dickstein

Picture Researcher   Diane Moroff

Senior Designer   Laurie Jewell

Designers   Michael Harvey, Teresa Clark

Cover Illustration   Alan J. Nahigian

Creative Director   Harold Steinberg

Copyright © 1988 by Chelsea House Publishers, a division of
Main Line Book Co. All rights reserved. Printed and bound
in the United States of America.

13   15   17   19   18   16   14   12

Library of Congress Cataloging in Publication Data
Russell, Sharman Apt.
   Frederick Douglass.

   (Black Americans of achievement)
   Bibliography: p.
   Includes index.
   1. Douglass, Frederick, 1817?–1895—Juvenile
literature.   2. Abolitionists—United States—Biography—
Juvenile literature.   3. Afro-Americans—Biography—
Juvenile literature. [1. Douglass, Frederick, 1817?–
1895.   2. Abolitionists.   3. Afro-Americans—Biography]
I. Title.   II. Series.
E449.D75R87   1988   973.8'092'4 [B]   [92]   87-17843
ISBN 1-55546-580-3
     0-7910-0204-7   (pbk.)

CONTENTS

BLACK AMERICANS OF ACHIEVEMENT

RALPH ABERNATHY
civil rights leader

MUHAMMAD ALI
heavyweight champion

RICHARD ALLEN
religious leader and social activist

LOUIS ARMSTRONG
musician

ARTHUR ASHE
tennis great

JOSEPHINE BAKER
entertainer

JAMES BALDWIN
author

BENJAMIN BANNEKER
scientist and mathematician

AMIRI BARAKA
poet and playwright

COUNT BASIE
bandleader and composer

ROMARE BEARDEN
artist

JAMES BECKWOURTH
frontiersman

MARY MCLEOD
BETHUNE
educator

BLANCHE BRUCE
politician

RALPH BUNCHE
diplomat

GEORGE WASHINGTON
CARVER
botanist

CHARLES CHESNUTT
author

BILL COSBY
entertainer

PAUL CUFFE
merchant and abolitionist

FATHER DIVINE
religious leader

FREDERICK DOUGLASS
abolitionist editor

CHARLES DREW
physician

W.E.B. DU BOIS
scholar and activist

PAUL LAURENCE DUNBAR
poet

KATHERINE DUNHAM
dancer and choreographer

MARIAN WRIGHT EDELMAN
civil rights leader and lawyer

DUKE ELLINGTON
bandleader and composer

RALPH ELLISON
author

JULIUS ERVING
basketball great

JAMES FARMER
civil rights leader

ELLA FITZGERALD
singer

MARCUS GARVEY
black-nationalist leader

DIZZY GILLESPIE
musician

PRINCE HALL
social reformer

W. C. HANDY
father of the blues

WILLIAM HASTIE
educator and politician

MATTHEW HENSON
explorer

CHESTER HIMES
author

BILLIE HOLIDAY
singer

JOHN HOPE
educator

LENA HORNE
entertainer

LANGSTON HUGHES
poet

ZORA NEALE HURSTON
author

JESSE JACKSON
civil rights leader and politician

JACK JOHNSON
heavyweight champion

JAMES WELDON JOHNSON
author

SCOTT JOPLIN
composer

BARBARA JORDAN
politician

MARTIN LUTHER KING, JR.
civil rights leader

ALAIN LOCKE
scholar and educator

JOE LOUIS
heavyweight champion

RONALD MCNAIR
astronaut

MALCOLM X
militant black leader

THURGOOD MARSHALL
Supreme Court justice

ELIJAH MUHAMMAD
religious leader

JESSE OWENS
champion athlete

CHARLIE PARKER
musician

GORDON PARKS
photographer

SIDNEY POITIER
actor

ADAM CLAYTON POWELL, JR.
political leader

LEONTYNE PRICE
opera singer

A. PHILIP RANDOLPH
labor leader

PAUL ROBESON
singer and actor

JACKIE ROBINSON
baseball great

BILL RUSSELL
basketball great

JOHN RUSSWURM
publisher

SOJOURNER TRUTH
antislavery activist

HARRIET TUBMAN
antislavery activist

NAT TURNER
slave revolt leader

DENMARK VESEY
slave revolt leader

MADAM C. J. WALKER
entrepreneur

BOOKER T. WASHINGTON
educator

HAROLD WASHINGTON
politician

WALTER WHITE
civil rights leader and author

RICHARD WRIGHT
author

ON ACHIEVEMENT

Coretta Scott King

BEFORE YOU BEGIN this book, I hope you will ask yourself what the word excellence means to you. I think that it's a question we should all ask, and keep asking as we grow older and change. Because the truest answer to it should never change. When you think of excellence, perhaps you think of success at work; or of becoming wealthy; or meeting the right person, getting married, and having a good family life.

Those important goals are worth striving for, but there is a better way to look at excellence. As Martin Luther King, Jr., said in one of his last sermons, "I want you to be first in love. I want you to be first in moral excellence. I want you to be first in generosity. If you want to be important, wonderful. If you want to be great, wonderful. But recognize that he who is greatest among you shall be your servant."

My husband, Martin Luther King, Jr., knew that the true meaning of achievement is service. When I met him, in 1952, he was already ordained as a Baptist preacher and was working towards a doctoral degree at Boston University. I was studying at the New England Conservatory and dreamed of accomplishments in music. We married a year later, and after I graduated the following year we moved to Montgomery, Alabama. We didn't know it then, but our notions of achievement were about to undergo a dramatic change.

You may have read or heard about what happened next. What began with the boycott of a local bus line grew into a national movement, and by the time he was assassinated in 1968 my husband had fashioned a black movement powerful enough to shatter forever the practice of racial segregation. What you may not have read about is where he got his method for resisting injustice without compromising his religious beliefs.

He got the strategy of nonviolence from a man of a different race, who lived in a distant country, and even practiced a different religion. The man was Mahatma Gandhi, the great leader of India, who devoted his life to serving humanity in the spirit of love and nonviolence. It was in these principles that Martin discovered his method for social reform. More than anything else, those two principles were the key to his achievements.

This book is about black Americans who served society through the excellence of their achievements. It forms a part of the rich history of black men and women in America—a history of stunning accomplishments in every field of human endeavor, from literature and art to science, industry, education, diplomacy, athletics, jurisprudence, even polar exploration.

Not all of the people in this history had the same ideals, but I think you will find something that all of them have in common. Like Martin Luther King, Jr., they all decided to become "drum majors" and serve humanity. In that principle—whether it was expressed in books, inventions, or song—they found something outside themselves to use as a goal and a guide. Something that showed them a way to serve others, instead of living only for themselves.

Reading the stories of these courageous men and women not only helps us discover the principles that we will use to guide our own lives, but it teaches us about our black heritage and about America itself. It is crucial for us to know the heroes and heroines of our history and to realize that the price we paid in our struggle for equality in America was dear. But we must also understand that we have gotten as far as we have partly because America's democratic system and ideals made it possible.

We still are struggling with racism and prejudice. But the great men and women in this series are a tribute to the spirit of our democratic ideals and the system in which they have flourished. And that makes their stories special, and worth knowing. ❧

FREDERICK DOUGLASS

1
THE
FORTUNATE
MEETING

—•◗•—

IN AUGUST 1841, a group of men and women gathered at the Atheneum hall on the island of Nantucket. They were members of the Massachusetts Anti-Slavery Society, and their goal was to abolish the inhumane system of slavery that existed throughout the southern United States, where millions of black people were held in bondage. The abolitionists, as those who were fighting against slavery were called, were morally opposed to the practice of buying and selling fellow human beings. They were determined that all people living in America should enjoy the rights to life, liberty, and the pursuit of happiness.

Among those attending the abolitionist meeting was Frederick Douglass, a young black man who had escaped from slavery in Maryland almost three years before. Tall, strong, with a thick mane of hair, the 23-year-old Douglass was strikingly handsome. Ever since he had gained his freedom, moved to the Massachusetts port town of New Bedford, and changed his name from Bailey to Douglass to hide his identity, he had attended meetings of the American Anti-Slavery Society and subscribed to the organization's newspaper, the *Liberator*. He also preached at a local black church, mixing biblical teachings with his reflections on the evils of slavery. A man who always seemed to be working, Douglass decided in the sum-

Shortly after fleeing from his life as a slave, 23-year-old Frederick Douglass joined the American Anti-Slavery Society as a traveling speaker.

An 1841 meeting of the American Anti-Slavery Society, which had been formed eight years earlier. The society was one of the leading forces in the abolitionist movement.

mer of 1841 to take a brief holiday and go to the meeting on Nantucket.

As Douglass sat waiting for the speakers to appear, he was not aware that his name had come to the attention of the leaders of the abolitionist movement. Most of the people in the hall were strangers to him. Consequently, he was amazed when William Coffin, an abolitionist from New Bedford, approached him and asked if he would address the crowd. Coffin had heard Douglass speak in church and was impressed by the intelligent, self-educated ex-slave. He was sure that Douglass's stories of his years as a slave named Frederick Bailey would have a strong effect on the audience.

Although Douglass accepted Coffin's invitation, he was so nervous that he could barely stand up. Once on the speaker's platform, the normally articulate young man stammered and hesitated. But his listeners called out to encourage him, and, little by little, Douglass was able to explain to them what it was like to be a slave. He told how he had been separated from his mother soon after birth. He told about the awful beatings he endured and about the times he had been overworked and passed out from exhaustion—and been beaten. But he also told how he had learned to read and write, how he had become a skilled tradesman, and how he had then escaped to freedom. And he told the audience how important the abolitionist movement was to former slaves like himself.

Douglass's words stirred up the New England crowd. Most of the people attending the meeting were white, and few had ever seen a slave or listened to a black person tell about his life. Deeply religious, they believed that owning slaves was sinful. But only a handful knew about the brutal conditions under which the majority of slaves lived. Many people in the North accepted statements made by southern slaveowners that blacks were inferior to whites, that they were

One of the most popular antislavery newspapers, The Liberator *was edited by abolitionist leader William Lloyd Garrison.*

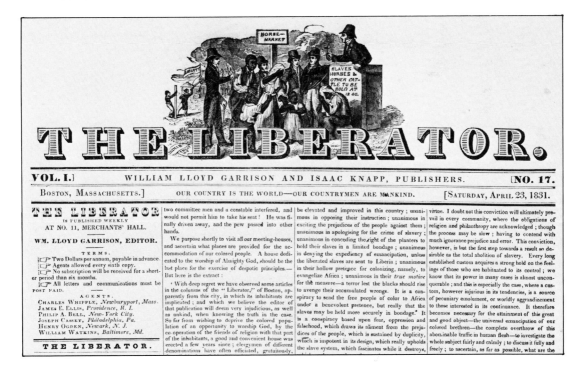

THE LIBERATOR.

VOL. I.]   WILLIAM LLOYD GARRISON AND ISAAC KNAPP, PUBLISHERS.   [NO. 17.

BOSTON, MASSACHUSETTS.]   OUR COUNTRY IS THE WORLD—OUR COUNTRYMEN ARE MANKIND.   [SATURDAY, APRIL 23, 1831.

THE LIBERATOR
IS PUBLISHED WEEKLY
AT NO. 11, MERCHANTS' HALL.

WM. LLOYD GARRISON, EDITOR.

TERMS.
☞ Two Dollars per annum, payable in advance.
☞ Agents allowed every sixth copy.
☞ No subscription will be received for a shorter period than six months.
☞ All letters and communications must be POST PAID.

AGENTS.
CHARLES WHIPPLE, *Newburyport, Mass.*
JAMES E. ELLIS, *Providence, R. I.*
PHILIP A. BELL, *New-York City.*
JOSEPH CASSEY, *Philadelphia, Pa.*
HENRY OGDEN, *Newark, N. J.*
WILLIAM WATKINS, *Baltimore, Md.*

THE LIBERATOR.

two committee men and a constable interfered, and would not permit him to take his seat! He was finally driven away, and the pew passed into other hands.

We purpose shortly to visit all our meeting-houses, and ascertain what places are provided for the accommodation of our colored people. A house dedicated to the worship of Almighty God, should be the last place for the exercise of despotic principles.—But here is the extract:

'With deep regret we have observed some articles in the columns of the "Liberator," of Boston, apparently from this city, in which its inhabitants are implicated; and which we believe the editor of that publication will deem very injudicious, as well as unkind, when knowing the truth in the case. So far from wishing to deprive the colored population of an opportunity to worship God, by the co-operation of the friends of religion with that part of the inhabitants, a good and convenient house was erected a few years since; clergymen of different denominations have often officiated, gratuitously,

be elevated and improved in this country; unanimous in opposing their instruction; unanimous in exciting the prejudices of the people against them; unanimous in conceding the right of the planters to hold their slaves in a limited bondage; unanimous in denying the expediency of emancipation, unless the liberated slaves are sent to Liberia; unanimous in their hollow pretence for colonizing, namely, to evangelize Africa; unanimous in their *true motive* for the measure—a terror lest the blacks should rise to avenge their accumulated wrongs. It is a conspiracy to send the free people of color to Africa under a benevolent pretence, but really that the slaves may be held more securely in bondage.* It is a conspiracy based upon fear, oppression and falsehood, which draws its aliment from the prejudices of the people, which is sustained by duplicity, which is impotent in its design, which really upholds the slave system, which fascinates while it destroys,

virtue. I doubt not this conviction will ultimately prevail in every community, where the obligations of religion and philanthropy are acknowledged; though the process may be slow; having to contend with much ignorance prejudice and error. This conviction, however, is but the first step towards a result so desirable as the total abolition of slavery. Every long established custom acquires a strong hold on the feelings of those who are habituated to its control; we know that its power in many cases is almost unconquerable; and this is especially the case, where a custom, however injurious in its tendencies, is a source of pecuniary emolument, or worldly aggrandizement to those interested in its continuance. It therefore becomes necessary for the attainment of this great and good object—the universal emancipation of our colored brethren—the complete overthrow of this abominable traffic in human flesh—to investigate the whole subject fairly and calmly; to discuss it fully and freely; to ascertain, as far as possible, what are the

Slaves were often shackled, along with being brutalized in other ways, so that their owners could keep them under control.

happy as slaves, and that they were ignorant and were good only for menial tasks and hard labor. But here was Frederick Douglass, a man who had been raised a slave and yet who stood before the audience proudly displaying the broad knowledge he had gained during his years of servitude. There could hardly be a better argument for black emancipation, or freedom, than Douglass's life story.

When Douglass finished his speech, the audience gave him a deafening round of applause, cheering him for all that he had accomplished in the face of such injustice. The abolitionists appreciated Douglass's courage in speaking to them, for though he lived in a state where slavery was illegal, under federal law he was still a fugitive slave. If his whereabouts became known, his former owner would be within his rights to send a slave hunter to kidnap Douglass and bring him back to Maryland in chains.

Douglass was followed on the speaker's platform by William Lloyd Garrison, one of the leading spokesmen of the abolitionist movement. Garrison was as thrilled by Douglass's words as everyone else in the hall. Never, he declared, had a person given a more moving speech in support of liberty. When he asked the abolitionists if they would ever allow Douglass to be returned to slavery, they shouted, "No." They promised to protect Douglass and other fugitive slaves, even if it meant breaking the law.

At the end of the meeting, Douglass agreed to take a position as a traveling agent of the American Anti-Slavery Society. During the next three years, he would speak in towns and cities throughout the northern United States. In some places he would win converts to the cause of black emancipation; in others, he would be beaten by hostile crowds. But he would carry on with his task, and in 1845, with the publication of the first of his autobiographical works,

Narrative of the Life of Frederick Douglass, an American Slave, he would become known throughout the world as a leader of the antislavery movement. As an editor, writer, and speaker, Douglass would play a major role in helping to end the ugly institution that divided his country between those who favored human freedom and those who relied on the forced labor of others.

Douglass's attendance at the Nantucket meeting was, as William Lloyd Garrison wrote in his preface to the *Narrative*, a "most fortunate occurrence. . . . Fortunate," he wrote, "for the cause of negro emancipation, and of universal liberty." Garrison was among the first to feel the powerful force of Douglass's attack on human bondage and was moved to write of that experience, "I think I never hated slavery so intensely as at that moment." Frederick Douglass would arouse this feeling in many people before his long struggle for black freedom and rights was over. ❧

2

FREEDOM'S RAINBOW

T HE SLAVE Frederick Bailey was born in February 1818 on Holmes Hill farm, near the town of Easton on Maryland's Eastern Shore. The farm was part of an estate owned by Aaron Anthony, a former ship's captain and the manager of the plantations belonging to Edward Lloyd V, one of the wealthiest men in Maryland. The main Lloyd plantation was near the eastern side of the Chesapeake Bay, 12 miles from Holmes Hill farm, and it was there, in a house he had built near the Lloyd mansion, that Frederick's first master lived.

Frederick's mother, tall, dark Harriet Bailey, worked in the cornfields surrounding Holmes Hill. It was from her that he got his last name. He knew little about his father except that the man was white—as a child he would hear rumors that the master himself, Captain Anthony, had sired him.

Because Harriet Bailey was required to work long hours in the fields, Frederick was separated from his mother soon after birth and was sent to live with his grandmother, Betsey Bailey. The mother of three sons and nine daughters, many of whom worked on Anthony's lands, Betsey Bailey lived in a cabin a

Slaves waiting to be sold at an auction—a practice that began in the American South shortly after the New World had been colonized.

17

A front-page illustration from the antislavery newspaper Emancipator *depicts a slave being separated from her child—just one of the many tragic aspects of slavery.*

short distance from Holmes Hill farm. Her job was to look after Harriet's children until they were old enough to work.

In his earliest years, Frederick did not think of himself as a slave. His mother visited him when she could, but he had only a hazy memory of her. He spent many happy days playing in the woods by his grandmother's cabin, and only gradually did he begin to learn about a mysterious person called Old Master, whose name Betsey Bailey spoke with fear.

One morning, when Frederick was about six years old, his grandmother told him that they were going on a long journey. They set off down the road leading westward, with Frederick clinging to his grandmother's skirts as they walked for mile after mile. Finally, the old woman and the boy reached a large, elegant house, around which were playing many children.

Frederick's grandmother pointed out to him his brother Perry and his sisters Sarah and Eliza among

The record of Douglass's birth to Harriet Bailey in February 1818. He later insisted, "I do not remember to have ever met a slave who could tell of his birthday."

the children in the yard. The boy was confused, not understanding who these people were, but he had a feeling that something bad was about to happen. When his grandmother told him to join the other children, he did so reluctantly, but he refused to play with them. After a while, one of the children ran up to Frederick and yelled at him that his grandmother was gone. He collapsed on the ground and wept. The happy years at his grandmother's cabin had ended.

Frederick would later write, "this was my first introduction to the realities of the slave system." More painful lessons were to follow. The slave children of Captain Anthony's household were fed cornmeal mush that was placed in a trough, to which they were called, Frederick later wrote, "like so many pigs." Using oyster shells and other homemade spoons, the hungry children competed with each other for every bit of the gruel. A linen shirt that hung to their knees was all that they were given to wear. None had beds

Captain Thomas Auld became Douglass's master shortly after the slave turned 15 years old. According to Douglass, "My master found religious sanction for his cruelty."

or warm blankets. They suffered miserably on cold winter nights, huddling in recesses in the kitchen of the Anthony house. "My feet have been so cracked with frost," Frederick noted later, "that the pen with which I am writing might be laid in the gashes."

One of Frederick's worst experiences was the first time he saw a whipping take place. One night he was woken by a woman's screams. Peering through a crack in the wall of the kitchen, he saw Captain Anthony lashing the bare back of Hester Bailey, Frederick's aunt, with a heavy cowskin whip. Terrified, Frederick forced himself to watch the woman's whole long ordeal. In the coming years, he was to see many slaves whipped by their masters. Occasionally, he himself would be the victim. Although some masters were relatively kind, others, like Captain Anthony, beat their slaves brutally if they did not obey orders quickly enough.

Because Frederick's mother worked 12 miles from the Lloyd plantation, she was rarely able to visit her children there. Frederick saw her for the last time when he was seven years old. He remembered her giving a severe scolding to the mean household cook who disliked Frederick and gave him little food. A few months after the visit, Harriet Bailey died, but Frederick did not learn about this until much later.

Overall, Frederick was luckier than most of the slave children. He had a natural charm that many people found engaging, and he was chosen to be the companion of Daniel Lloyd, the youngest son of the plantation's owner. Frederick's chief friend and protector was Lucretia Auld, Aaron Anthony's daughter, who had recently married a ship's captain named Thomas Auld. She seemed to think that Frederick was a special child.

One day in 1826, Lucretia Auld told Frederick that he was being sent to live with her brother-in-law, Hugh Auld, who managed a ship-building firm in Baltimore, Maryland. She told him that if he scrubbed himself clean, she would give him a pair of trousers. Frederick was overjoyed at this chance to escape the life of a field hand. He cleaned himself and won his first pair of pants. Within three days he was on his way to the busy port of Baltimore.

At first Frederick got along extremely well with his new masters. Sophia, Hugh Auld's wife, had never owned a slave before and did not know the "proper" way to treat one. She disliked the servile manners that Frederick had been taught on the plantation, and she told him to look her in the eye when he spoke to her. Frederick's only jobs were to run errands and care for and entertain the Aulds' infant son, Tommy. It was pleasant work for Frederick, and he grew to love the little boy.

A prized possession for a former slave in colonial America: a certificate showing that he has been declared a free man.

This illustration shows a slave store in the South. Domestic servants waiting to be sold were often made to wear their best clothes so as to attract buyers.

A religious woman, Sophia Auld frequently read aloud from the Bible. Intrigued, Frederick asked his mistress to teach him how to read, and she readily consented. He soon mastered the alphabet and a few simple words. Proud of her pupil's progress, Sophia Auld told her husband what she had done. Hugh Auld was furious. Teaching a slave to read was unlawful, he said. It made a slave unfit for his work—namely, obeying his master without question or thought. A slave who knew how to read and write could forge papers that said he was free and then escape to one of the states in the North, where slavery was outlawed.

Sophia Auld heeded her husband's orders and stopped the lessons. But Frederick had learned a great deal from Hugh Auld's outburst. If learning how to read and write made him unfit to be a slave and was the pathway to freedom, then gaining this knowledge would be his goal. Once in command of the alphabet, he progressed quickly on his own. He made friends with poor white children he met on his errands and used them as teachers, paying for his reading lessons with pieces of bread.

At home, Frederick read parts of books and newspapers when he could, but he had to be constantly on guard against his mistress. Sophia Auld had taken the words of her husband to heart, and she screamed at Frederick whenever she saw him looking at reading material. The change in his mistress troubled Frederick, who began to see that slavery was a "fatal poison" for the owner as well as the slave. As he wrote later about Sophia Auld, "She at first regarded me as a child, like any other. . . . When she came to consider me as property, our relations to each other changed."

However, Frederick gradually learned both how to read and write. While doing small jobs at Hugh

Douglass first learned how to read under the guidance of Sophia Auld. However, these lessons were soon stopped by her husband, who feared that education would make Douglass unfit to be a slave.

Douglass often found slaveowners to be hypocritical in their actions. They would profess to be God-abiding, yet their treatment of their slaves was certainly less than angelic.

Auld's shipyard, he watched the workmen label timbers and masts with letters to indicate where the pieces would be used. Frederick copied these letters and soon learned how to write whole words. With a little money he earned doing errands, he bought a copy of *The Columbian Orator*, a collection of speeches and essays dealing with liberty, democracy, and courage. In one of the pieces, a master and his slave discuss the institution of slavery, and they finally agree that it is wrong to hold another man in bondage.

Frederick was strongly affected by the speeches on freedom in *The Columbian Orator*, and by reading the local newspapers he began to learn about abolitionists—men and women who were fighting to end slavery in the United States. He also read about the slave rebellion led by Nat Turner in Virginia in 1831. The fiery preacher Turner organized an army of slaves that went on a rampage, massacring all the slaveholders in its path. Federal and state troops finally crushed the uprising, but many American slaves honored Turner as a great freedom fighter.

Not yet 13 years old but afire with new ideas that both tormented and inspired him, Frederick began to loathe slavery with a passion. "I had penetrated to the secret of all slavery and oppression," he wrote. "Slaveholders are only a band of successful robbers." His dreams of emancipation were encouraged by the example of other blacks in Baltimore, most of whom were free. But new laws passed by southern state legislatures had made it increasingly difficult for owners to free their slaves.

During this time, Aaron Anthony died, and his property fell to his two sons and his daughter, Lucretia Auld. Frederick was still part of the Anthony estate, and so he was sent back to the Lloyd plantation to be part of the division of property. Lined up beside his brothers, sisters, aunts, and cousins to be ranked and valued with the horses, sheep, and pigs, Frederick prayed that he would not be chosen by the captain's eldest son, the cruel drunkard Andrew Anthony. The man had already wasted much of his inheritance, and any slave chosen by him was likely to be sold to slave traders and taken to Georgia, Alabama, or another state in the Deep South, where it would be nearly impossible for a slave to gain his freedom.

Fortunately, Frederick was selected by Thomas and Lucretia Auld and was sent back to Hugh and Sophia Auld in Baltimore. Seeing his family divided up strengthened his hatred of slavery, however, and he was especially upset that his grandmother, considered to be too old for any work, was turned out of her cabin and sent into the woods to die.

Within a year of Frederick's return to Baltimore, Lucretia Auld died. The two Auld brothers then got

Douglass said of his life as a slave, "We were worked in all weathers. It was never too hot or too cold; it could never rain, blow, hail, or snow, too hard for us to work in the field."

into a dispute, and Thomas wrote to Hugh demanding the return of his late wife's property, which included Frederick. Frederick was sorry to leave Baltimore. He had recently become a teacher to a group of other young blacks. In addition, a black preacher named Charles Lawson had adopted him as a spiritual son, telling the young man that he was destined to become a religious leader. But unlike these men, Frederick was a slave, and in March 1833, the 15-year-old was forced to leave his friends behind and go to Thomas Auld's new farm near the town of Saint Michaels, a few miles from the Lloyd plantation.

Frederick was extremely unhappy with his new situation as a field hand on the farm. Thomas Auld starved his slaves, and they had to steal food from neighboring farms to stay alive. The sullen Frederick received many beatings, and he saw worse ones given to an awkward slave whose hands had been crippled in a fire. He organized a Sunday religious service for the slaves in the area, but the group met in Saint Michaels only a few times before it was broken up by a mob led by Thomas Auld.

Frederick had little liking for white clergymen, for they preached that it was a slave's duty to obey his master. But the hypocrisy of his master, who was known as one of the most devout men in the neighborhood, appalled Frederick. Thomas Auld whipped his slaves while reading from the Bible. A bad manager, he knew little about farming, and he found Frederick especially difficult to control. At last, Auld decided to have someone tame his unruly slave for him.

In January 1834, Frederick was sent to work for Edward Covey, a poor farmer who had gained a reputation around Saint Michaels for being a skilled "slave breaker." Covey seldom needed to rent field hands because richer farmers loaned him their slaves so that he could train them to be obedient workers.

Frederick was not entirely displeased with the new arrangement because Covey fed his slaves better than Auld did.

Like the other slaves on Covey's farm, Frederick worked from dawn until after nightfall, plowing, hoeing, and picking corn. Although the men were given plenty of food, they were allowed only a few minutes to gobble it down before they were forced to return to their muscle-breaking, mind-breaking, heart-breaking labor. They always had to be on the lookout for Covey because he hid behind bushes and spied on them as they worked. When the farmer caught a slave resting, he would beat him with thick branches.

After only one week on the farm, Frederick let an oxen team run wild and was given a serious beating by Covey. During the following months, he was continually whipped until he began to feel that he was indeed broken. On a hot afternoon in August, his strength finally failed him and he collapsed in the dirt. Covey kicked and beat him—to no avail—and then stalked off in disgust. Frederick at last managed to get up and walk to the Auld farm, where he pleaded

This illustration shows a fugitive slave being returned to his owners in the South. Although slavery itself was illegal in the North, it was legal for a slave found hiding in a free state to be returned to his owner.

with his master to let him stay. However, Auld had little sympathy for his desperate slave and sent him back to Covey.

Beaten down though he was, Frederick found the strength to rebel when Covey began tying him to a post in preparation for another whipping. "At that moment—from whence came the spirit I don't know— I resolved to fight," Frederick wrote. "I seized Covey hard by the throat, and as I did so, I rose." The two men battled for almost two hours. Covey finally gave up, telling Frederick that he would have been whipped less severely if he had not resisted. "The truth was," said Frederick, "that he had not whipped me at all."

Frederick had discovered an important truth: "Men are whipped oftenest who are whipped easiest." He was lucky; legally, a slave could be killed for resisting his master. But Covey had a reputation to protect and did not want it known that he could not control a 16-year-old boy. Frederick was never beaten during the rest of his time on Covey's farm.

After a year's service with Covey, Frederick was sent to work for a farmer named William Freeland, a relatively kind master. But by now Frederick wanted more than kindness; he wanted his freedom. He started an illegal school for blacks in the area that met secretly at night and on Sundays, and with five other slaves he began to plot an escape to the North.

After working for a year on Freeland's farm, Frederick was ready to leave. His group planned to steal a boat, row to the northern tip of Chesapeake Bay, and then flee on foot to the free state of Pennsylvania. However, just before the Easter holiday in 1836, when the escape was supposed to take place, a band of armed white men seized the slaves and threw them in jail. One of Frederick's associates had exposed the plot.

Frederick was imprisoned for about a week. While in jail, he was inspected by slave traders, and he fully

An advertisement announcing the arrival of a shipload of 250 men and women to be sold into slavery.

expected that he would be sold to "a life of living death" in the Deep South. To his surprise, Thomas Auld came and released him. Then, instead of shipping his unmanageable slave to the Alabama cotton fields, Frederick's master sent him back to Hugh Auld in Baltimore. The two brothers had finally settled their dispute.

More than three years had passed since Frederick had left Baltimore. The 18 year old was now 6 feet tall and very strong from his days in the fields. Hugh Auld decided that Frederick should earn his keep by working as a caulker—a man who forced sealing matter into the seams in a boat's hull to make it watertight. He was hired out to a local shipbuilder so that he could learn the trade.

While apprenticing at the shipyard, Frederick was harassed by white workers who did not want blacks—no matter whether they were slaves or freemen—competing with them for jobs. One afternoon, a group of white apprentices beat up Frederick and nearly took out one of his eyes. Hugh Auld was angry when he saw what had happened to his slave, and he attempted to press charges against Frederick's assailants. However, none of the shipyard's white employees would step forward and testify about the beating, so the case had to be dropped. Free blacks had little hope of obtaining justice through the southern court system, which refused to accept a black person's testimony against a white person. A slave like Frederick had no chance at all.

After Frederick recovered from his injuries, he began apprenticing at the shipyard where Hugh Auld worked. Within a year, he was an experienced caulker and was being paid the highest wages possible for a tradesman at his level. He was allowed to seek his own employment and collect his own pay, and at the end of each week he gave all his earnings to Hugh Auld. Sometimes his master would let him keep a little money, but as time passed, the hardworking young man became more and more vexed that he was being robbed of his wages. Freedom seemed to be tantalizingly out of reach.

Still, life had improved dramatically for the former field hand. In his spare time, he met with a group of educated free blacks and indulged in the luxury of being a student again. Some of the free blacks formed an educational association called the East Baltimore Mental Improvement Society, to which they graciously admitted the slave Frederick Bailey. Here he honed his debating skills.

At one of the society's gatherings, Frederick met a free black woman named Anna Murray. A few years older than Frederick, Anna was a servant for a wealthy Baltimore family. Although a plain, uneducated woman, she was thrifty, industrious, and religious. Anna and Frederick were soon in love, and by 1838 they were engaged.

Douglass first sensed what it must be like to live as a free man when he was hired out as a worker at the shipyard in Baltimore, Maryland.

By Jacob Radcliff Mayor, and Richard Riker
Recorder, of the City of New-York.

It is hereby Certified, That pursuant to the statute in such case made and provided, we have this day examined *one* certain Male Negro Slave named *George* the property of *Wm D Chay*

which slave *is* about to be manumitted, and *he* appearing to us to be under forty-five years of age, and of sufficient ability to provide *for himself* we have granted this Certificate, this *time & fourth* day of *April* in the year of our Lord, one thousand eight hundred and *four teen*

Jacob Radcliff

R Riker

Register's Office Lib no 2 of Manumissions page 62
Wm S Slocum Register

A signed certificate of manumission, announcing one's formal emancipation from slavery, was a much-coveted document.

Love and courtship only spurred Frederick's discontent with his status. "Give a man a bad master," he wrote later, "and he aspires to a good master; give him a good master and he aspires to be his own master." After Frederick's escape attempt, Thomas Auld had promised him that if he worked hard he would be freed when he was 25 years old. But Frederick did not trust his master, and he resolved to escape. This was very difficult, however; professional slave catchers patrolled the roads on the borders between the slave and free states, and free blacks traveling by rail or steamboat had to carry official papers listing their name, age, height, skin color, and other distinguishing features.

In order to escape, Frederick had to get more money to pay for traveling expenses. Frederick arranged with Hugh Auld to hire out his time; that is, Frederick agreed to take care of his own room and board and to pay his master a set amount each week, keeping any extra money for himself. This gave him an incentive to work harder and allowed him his first taste of living on his own.

For a few months all went well, and Frederick's savings grew. He began to study the violin and met with his friends at social gatherings held far outside the city. One day he returned late from one of these meetings and failed to pay Hugh Auld on time. Auld was enraged and revoked his hiring-out privilege. Equally angry, Frederick refused to work for a week. He finally gave in to Auld's threats, but he also made a firm resolution: three weeks hence, on September 3, 1838, he would be on a northbound train.

The decision was a difficult one for Frederick, and it was a mark of his character that he pursued escape so doggedly. He was going to be leaving his friends and his fairly comfortable life in Baltimore forever. He did not know when he would get to see Anna Murray again. Furthermore, if he was caught while escaping, he was sure that he would be killed or sold to slave traders. None of this weakened his resolve.

With money borrowed from Anna, Frederick bought a ticket to Philadelphia, Pennsylvania. He also had a friend's "sailor's protection," a document that certified that the person named on it was a free seaman. Dressed in a sailor's red shirt and black cravat, he transformed himself from the slave Frederick Bailey to a free man of the sea.

Furtively boarding the train just as it started to move, Frederick reached northern Maryland before the conductor came to the "Negro car" to collect tickets and examine papers. This was a tense moment for Frederick because he did not fit the description on the paper he carried. But with only a quick glance, the conductor walked on, and the relieved Frederick sank back in his seat. He stayed on guard throughout the rest of the trip as the train passed through the slave state of Delaware. On a couple of occasions, he thought that he had been recognized by other passengers from Baltimore, but if so they did not betray him.

At Wilmington, Delaware, Frederick boarded a steamboat to Philadelphia. Even after stepping on Pennsylvania's free soil, he knew he was not yet safe from roving slave catchers. He immediately inquired about directions to New York City, and that night he took another train north. On September 4, 1838, he merged with the crowds bustling "to and fro between the lofty walls of Broadway in New York."

Frederick never quite found the words to describe his feelings at leaving behind his life in slavery. "A new world had opened upon me," he wrote later. "Anguish and grief, like darkness and rain, may be depicted, but gladness and joy, like the rainbow, defy the skill of pen or pencil."

$200 REWARD!

Ran away from his owner [a Lady residing near Upper Marlboro, Prince George's County, Md.] on or about the 12th inst. of this month, a bright Mullatto man named Frank, a carpenter by trade, he is about five feet 9 or 10 inches high, light grey eyes, slow in speech, and very good personal appearance, about twenty-five years of age, his clothing good.

One Hundred dollars will be paid if apprehended within thirty miles of home, if more than thirty, the above reward, provided he be secured in Jail so that his owner gets him again.

W. D. BOWIE,
for the owner,
Buena Vista Post Office, Prince George's Co. Md.
February 14th, 1853.

An advertisement of a reward for the capture of a runaway slave. Douglass had been planning to escape to the North as early as 1836.

3

A
SOUL ON
FIRE

ALONE IN NEW YORK, Frederick quickly discovered that being free did not mean being free of cares. From a man he met on the street, he learned that southern slave catchers were roaming the city and hunting for fugitives in the boarding houses that accepted blacks. No one—black or white—was to be trusted.

After hearing this depressing news, Frederick wandered around the city for days, afraid to seek shelter or employment. Finally, he told an honest-looking black sailor about his circumstances. The man took him to David Ruggles, an officer in the New York Vigilance Committee. Ruggles and his associates were the city's link in the underground railroad, the network of people who harbored runaway slaves and helped transport them to safe areas in the northern United States and Canada.

Secure for the moment in Ruggles's home, Frederick sent for his fiancée, Anna Murray. The two were married on September 15, 1838. Ruggles told Frederick that in the port of New Bedford, Massachusetts, a center of the American whaling industry, he would be safe from slave catchers and he could find work as a caulker. Anna and Frederick took a steamer north. Upon arriving in New Bedford, they settled in the home of the well-to-do black family of Nathan Johnson.

The cover to "The Fugitive's Song," a musical composition published in 1845 honoring Douglass's escape from slavery.

CAUTION!!

COLORED PEOPLE

OF BOSTON, ONE & ALL,

You are hereby respectfully **CAUTIONED** and advised, to avoid conversing with the

Watchmen and Police Officers of Boston,

For since the recent **ORDER OF THE MAYOR & ALDERMEN,** they are empowered to act as

KIDNAPPERS

AND

Slave Catchers,

And they have already been actually employed in **KIDNAPPING, CATCHING, AND KEEPING SLAVES.** Therefore, if you value your **LIBERTY,** and the *Welfare of the Fugitives* among you, *Shun* them in every possible manner, as so many *HOUNDS* on the track of the most unfortunate of your race.

Keep a Sharp Look Out for KIDNAPPERS, and have TOP EYE open.

APRIL 24, 1851.

An advertisement warns blacks in Boston, Massachusetts, to be on the lookout for slave catchers hunting for fugitives in the area.

To go along with his new life, Frederick decided he should have a new name that would make it more difficult for slave catchers to trace him. Nathan Johnson was at the time reading *The Lady of the Lake*, a novel by the popular Scottish author Sir Walter Scott, and he suggested that Frederick name himself after a character in the book. Frederick Bailey thus became Frederick Douglass.

Once settled, Douglass was amazed to find that his neighbors in the North were wealthier than most slaveholders in Maryland. He had expected that northerners would be as poor as the people in the South who could not afford slaves. Many free blacks, such as Nathan Johnson, lived better than Thomas Auld or Edward Covey. On the New Bedford wharves, he saw how industry worked when it did not depend on enslaved human muscle: in loading a ship, 5 men and an ox did what it took 20 men to do in a southern port. Northern businesses made extensive use of labor-saving mechanical devices. To Douglass's eye, men who neither held a whip nor submitted to it worked more quietly and efficiently than those who did.

Still, New Bedford was not a paradise. Although black and white children attended the same schools, some public lecture halls were closed to blacks. Churches welcomed black worshipers but forced them to sit in separate sections, a practice that reinforced Douglass's already strong disillusionment with white clergymen. Worst of all, white shipyard employees would not allow skilled black tradesmen, such as Douglass, to work beside them.

Unable to find a job as a caulker, Douglass had to work as a common laborer. He sawed wood, shoveled coal, dug cellars, and loaded and unloaded ships. For a while, he operated a bellows in a brass foundry, where he nailed a newspaper to a nearby post so that he could read while he worked. Anna Douglass worked too as a household servant and laundress. In June

1839, she gave birth to their first child, a daughter named Rosetta. A son, Lewis, was born the following year.

Douglass had been living in New Bedford for only a few months when a young man approached him and asked if he wanted to subscribe to the *Liberator*, the newspaper edited by the outspoken leader of the American Anti-Slavery Society, William Lloyd Garrison. Douglass immediately became caught up in the *Liberator*'s weekly attacks on southern slaveholders. "The paper became my meat and my drink," wrote Douglass. "My soul was set all on fire."

Inevitably, Douglass became absorbed in the abolitionist movement, regularly attending lectures in New Bedford. The American Anti-Slavery Society, of which he was a member, had been formed in Philadelphia in 1833. Like Garrison, most of the leaders in the society were white, and black abolitionists sometimes had a difficult time making their voices

This illustration shows a slave being shipped to the North via the underground railroad. Originated by Reverend Charles T. Torrey, the underground railroad was a preplanned route that conveyed runaways to freedom in the northern states and in Canada.

Clandestine religious meetings (such as the one shown here) were held throughout America in the 1830s and 1840s. Many of these people joined the abolitionist movement out of religious conviction.

heard within the movement. Nonetheless, the black leaders kept up a constant battle to reduce racial prejudice in the North.

Douglass also became heavily involved in the affairs of the local black community, and he served as a preacher at the black Zion Methodist Church. Among the many issues he became involved in was the battle against attempts by white southerners to force blacks to move to Africa. Some free blacks had moved to Liberia, a settlement area established for them in West Africa in 1822. Douglass and many others in the abolitionist movement were opposed to African colonization schemes, believing that the United States was the true home of black Americans. A March 1839 issue of the *Liberator* carried some of Douglass's anticolonization statements.

At an abolitionist meeting in New Bedford in August 1841, the 23-year-old Douglass saw his hero,

William Lloyd Garrison, for the first time. A few days later, Douglass spoke before the crowd attending the annual meeting of the Massachusetts branch of the American Anti-Slavery Society. Garrison immediately recognized Douglass's potential as a speaker, and he was hired to be an agent for the society. As a traveling lecturer accompanying other abolitionist agents on tours of the northern states, his job was to talk about his life and to sell subscriptions to the *Liberator* and another newspaper, the *Anti-Slavery Standard*. His salary was more than he could make as a laborer, but more importantly, he was doing work that he believed in with all his heart and soul.

For most of the next 10 years, Douglass was associated with the Garrisonian school of the antislavery movement. A pacifist who believed that only moral persuasion could end slavery, Garrison attempted through his writings to educate slaveholders about the evils of the system they supported. He was opposed to slave uprisings and other violent resistance, but he was firm in his belief that slavery must be immediately and totally abolished. In the first issue of the *Liberator* in 1831, he had written:

> On this subject I do not wish to think, or speak, or write with moderation. . . . Tell a man whose house is on fire to give a moderate alarm; tell him to moderately rescue his wife from the hands of a ravisher . . . but urge me not to use moderation in a cause like the present. . . . I will not retreat a single inch— AND I WILL BE HEARD.

Ever controversial, Garrison made many enemies throughout the country. Because churches refused to take a stand against slavery, he made sweeping attacks on organized religion. He also believed that the U.S. Constitution upheld slavery, for it stated that nonfree individuals (slaves) should be counted as three-fifths of a person in the census figures used for determining a state's share of the national taxes and its number

Abolitionist leader William Lloyd Garrison attempted to combine slave emancipation with religious resurrection. "Genuine Abolition," he wrote, "is an essential part of Christianity, and aside from it there can be no humanity."

The American Anti-Slavery Society continued to meet once the Civil War had ended, for many of its members believed that slavery was not over until blacks had gained the right to vote.

of seats in the House of Representatives. Because the American government was so ill founded, Garrison said, abolitionists should refuse to vote or run for political office. He also called for the Union to be dissolved, demanding that it be split between a free nation in the North and a slavehold confederacy in the South.

Another cause that Garrison supported was political equality for women, and he fought to make it a part of the abolitionist program. Some men in the movement were opposed to him on this issue, and others thought that it distracted attention from the struggle against slavery. In 1840, when he insisted that women be allowed to serve as delegates to abolitionist conventions, much of the membership of the American Anti-Slavery Society split off and formed a separate organization. The new group, the Foreign and American Anti-Slavery Society, was not opposed to working with political organizations, and many of its members supported the small, newly formed antislavery Liberty party.

Although the often abrasive Garrison splintered the antislavery movement, he was a powerful leader. His sincerity and passionate devotion to the abolitionist cause impressed many men and women, and his views had a strong effect on Douglass. For three months in 1841, the ex-slave traveled with other abolitionists to lectures at meeting halls throughout Massachusetts. Introduced as "a piece of property" or "a graduate from that peculiar institution, with his diploma written on his back," he launched into stirring recollections of his years in slavery. Many of his friends in New Bedford thought the publicity was dangerous for him, but he was careful to omit details that would identify him as the fugitive slave Frederick Bailey.

On the lecture circuit, Douglass was an immediate success. "As a speaker, he has few equals," proclaimed

American Anti-Slavery Almanac for 1840.

The seven cuts following, are selected from thirteen, which may be found in the Anti-Slavery Almanac for 1840. They represent well-authenticated facts, and illustrate in various ways, the cruelties daily inflicted upon three millions of native born Americans, by their fellow-countrymen! A brief explanation follows each cut.

The peculiar " Domestic Institutions of our Southern brethren."

Selling a Mother from her Child.

Mothers with young Children at work in the field.

A Woman chained to a Girl, and a Man in irons at work in the field.

" They can't take care of themselves"; explained in an interesting article.

A group of illustrations appearing on the front page of the antislavery newspaper Emancipator *depicts the cruelties of slavery.*

Along with fighting for the emancipation of slaves, Douglass joined in the battle for women to receive the right to vote.

the Concord, Massachusetts, *Herald of Freedom*. The newspaper praised his skill in debating, his rich voice, and his elegant use of words. "He has wit, arguments, sarcasm, pathos—all that first rate men show in their master efforts." His flashing eyes, large mass of hair, and tall figure added to his performance.

Douglass's early speeches dealt mainly with his own experiences. With dramatic effect, he told stories about the brutal beatings given by slaveowners to women, children, and elderly people. He described how he had felt the head of a young girl and found it "nearly covered with festering sores." He told about masters "breeding" their female slaves. But he also used humor, making his audiences laugh out loud when he told how he broke the slave breaker Edward Covey. He especially delighted in imitating clergymen who warned slaves that they would be offending God if they disobeyed their masters.

The stories that Douglass told were just what his audiences wanted to hear. At the time, a flood of proslavery propaganda had been loosed by southern writers to combat abolitionist literature. According to these accounts, most slaves were content with their easy life. Supposedly, slaves worked only until noon, dressed and ate better than most poor whites, and enjoyed job security that would be envied by most northern factory workers. Many people in the North were taken in by the slaveholders' fictions, and abolitionists were often harassed by hostile mobs. Douglass's life story refuted the proslavery accounts; even so, he declared, his years in bondage would be deemed blissful by many slaves laboring in the Deep South.

After a few months of speaking, Douglass began to insert comments about the racial situation in the North. He reminded his audiences that even in Massachusetts a black man could not always find work in his chosen profession. Prejudice against blacks was still very strong in New England. He described how he had been thrown out of railroad cars restricted to whites. Even here, he said, churches segregated their congregations and offered blacks a second place in heaven.

After Douglass's first trial period as a lecturer was over, the abolitionists asked him to continue with his work, and he eagerly agreed. During 1842, he traveled throughout Massachusetts and New York in the company of William Lloyd Garrison and other prominent speakers. He also visited Rhode Island, helping to defeat a measure that would have extended voting rights to poor whites while denying them to blacks.

Late in 1842, Douglass became involved in the case of a fugitive slave in Boston who was about to be returned to his owner. He wrote a letter to a local newspaper that helped marshal support for the runaway, and the man was eventually bought from his owner by local citizens. In 1843, Douglass participated in the Hundred Conventions project, the American Anti-Slavery Society's six-month tour of meeting halls in Indiana, Ohio, Illinois, and other states in what was then the American West.

Although Douglass enjoyed his work as an antislavery agent, his job was not all applause and glory. Traveling lecturers had to live with poor accommodations. Douglass was often roughly handled when he refused to sit in the "Negro" sections of trains and steamships. Worst of all, abolitionist meetings in western states were sometimes disrupted by proslavery mobs. In Pendleton, Indiana, Douglass's hand was broken when he and a companion were beaten up by a gang of armed thugs. Such scenes were not all that uncommon on the western frontier, where abolitionists were often viewed as dangerous fanatics. In 1837, an abolitionist publisher, the Reverend Elijah Lovejoy, had been shot dead and his newspaper office burned down by a proslavery mob in Alton, Illinois.

Opponents of slave emancipation take action: the offices of abolitionist Elijah Lovejoy's antislavery newspaper in Alton, Illinois, are burned by a jeering mob in the late 1830s.

This engraving from 1856 shows a free black being expelled from a railway car reserved for whites only.

Despite such incidents, Douglass was sure that he had found his place in life. His abilities as a speaker grew even greater as he continued to lecture in 1844. Many abolitionists thought he was growing in ability a bit too quickly and that audiences were no longer as sympathetic to him. As early as 1841, friends had urged him to "keep a little of the plantation speech . . . it is not best that you seem too learned." They advised that he stick to talking about his life as a slave and leave debates about the goals of the antislavery movement to men like Garrison. Some abolitionists were probably envious of his success, but others were genuinely concerned that his brilliant rise was lessening his usefulness as an agent of the antislavery movement.

To some extent, the fear proved to be correct. People gradually began to doubt that Douglass was telling the truth about himself. Reporting on a lecture that he gave in 1844, the *Liberator* wrote that many people in the audience refused to believe his stories: "How a man, only six years out of bondage, and who had never gone to school a day in his life could speak with such eloquence—with such precision of language and power of thought—they were utterly at a loss to devise." Douglass himself told of how, when walking up to the speaker's platform, he would hear people whisper, "He's never been a slave, I'll warrant you."

His reputation at stake, Douglass decided on a dangerous course. He proposed to publish the story of his life. During the winter of 1844–45, he set down on paper all the facts—the actual names of the people and places connected with his years in slavery. When the proud author showed the finished manuscript to the abolitionist leader Wendell Phillips, his friend suggested that Douglass throw it in the fire before he was shipped back to Maryland. But Douglass was adamant. Even if Thomas Auld and every southern

NARRATIVE

OF THE

LIFE

OF

FREDERICK DOUGLASS,

AN

AMERICAN SLAVE.

WRITTEN BY HIMSELF.

BOSTON:
PUBLISHED AT THE ANTI-SLAVERY OFFICE,
No. 25 CORNHILL
1845.

slave catcher learned who he was, the rest of the world would hear his story too.

In May 1845, 5,000 copies of the *Narrative of the Life of Frederick Douglass, an American Slave* came off the press. William Lloyd Garrison and Wendell Phillips wrote introductions to the book, the former ending his piece with his motto, "No compromise with slavery! No union with slaveholders!" Almost immediately, Douglass's autobiography became a bestseller. Seven years after he boarded a train to freedom, he was truly in the public spotlight. ✺

The original title page of Douglass's autobiography, Narrative of the Life of Frederick Douglass, an American Slave, *which became a bestseller almost immediately upon publication.*

4
THE
CHATTEL BECOMES
A MAN

Addressing an English audience during his visit to London in 1846, Douglass spoke against a war between England and the United States even though, he said, "a war between them would eventuate in the emancipation of three millions of my brethren who are now held in most cruel bonds."

THE TREMENDOUS success enjoyed by Douglass's *Narrative* after its publication in 1845 was due in large part to its moral force. His book is a story of the triumph of dignity, courage, and self-reliance over the evils of the brutal, degrading slave system. It is more than an autobiography; it is a sermon on how slavery corrupts the human spirit and robs both master and slave of their freedom.

The *Narrative* enjoyed widespread popularity in the North, and European editions also sold very well. Douglass's fame as an author threatened his freedom, however. Federal laws gave Thomas Auld every right to seize his property, the fugitive slave Frederick Bailey. Fear of losing his liberty prompted Douglass to pursue a dream he had long held; in the summer of 1845 he decided to go to England. There he would be safe from slave catchers, and he would have the chance to speak to English audiences and try to win support for the American antislavery movement. In 1833, the British had passed a law granting a gradual emancipation to all slaves within the British Empire, and by 1838 all were free. The vigor of the English abolition movement was still strong.

As the wife of a traveling lecturer, Anna Douglass had probably grown used to her husband's long absences. By August 1845, the Douglasses had 4 children: 6-year-old Rosetta, 5-year-old Lewis,

47

Uneducated yet industrious, Anna Murray met Douglass at a gathering of the East Baltimore Mental Improvement Society. They were married in New York several years later, on September 15, 1838.

3-year-old Frederick, and 10-month-old Charles. The hardworking Anna not only raised the children but also toiled in a shoe factory in Lynn, Massachusetts, where the Douglasses had moved in 1842. Anna earned enough at her job to support the family while her husband was away.

Douglass sailed to England on the British steamship *Cambria*. He was forced to stay in the steerage (second class) area of the ship, but he made many friends on board and was even asked by the captain to give a lecture on slavery. Some young men in the audience were so angry about Douglass's speech that they threatened to toss him overboard. However, the captain told the men that he would put them in irons if they caused any trouble. The rest of the voyage was peaceful.

For nearly two years, Douglass traveled throughout the British Isles. Everywhere he went, prominent people welcomed him to their homes. Everywhere he spoke, enthusiastic crowds came to hear the fugitive slave denounce the system under which he had grown up. He was happy in his new surroundings, free of any feeling of being a chattel—a piece of property such as a slave. As he wrote to William Lloyd Garrison in January 1846, "Instead of the bright blue sky of America, I am covered with the soft gray fog of the Emerald Isle. I breathe and lo! The chattel becomes a man. I gaze around in vain for one who will question my equal humanity, claim me as a slave, or offer me an insult." He was astonished that he encountered so little racial prejudice among the British.

The chief topic of Douglass's lectures was, of course, slavery, but he also discussed a number of other causes that had become important to him. While in Dublin, Ireland, he spoke out in favor of the temperance movement, which was trying to stop the consumption of alcoholic drinks. Douglass himself pledged to abstain from alcohol in the future. As a young man,

"Nothing is more evident than that as slavery becomes strong, the pretensions of slaveholders range higher and broader," Douglass insisted.

TEMPTED.   PERSUADED.   HARDENED.   WRECKED.

THE PROGRESS OF INTEMPERANCE.

This lithograph shows the evils of intemperance. Douglass spoke out against the dangers of alcohol after witnessing how intoxication weakened many slaves.

he had hated the way slaveowners had encouraged their workers to drink themselves into a stupor during Christmas holidays. He saw alcohol as another means used by masters to humiliate their slaves. During his stay in Ireland, he also met with Daniel O'Connell, the Irish Catholic leader who was fighting to end British rule in his country. Douglass spoke out in favor of Irish independence.

In the summer of 1846, Douglass was joined by William Lloyd Garrison, and they traveled around England as a powerful team of antislavery lecturers. In Scotland, they became involved in a campaign against the Free Church of Scotland. The church was in part supported by contributions from American slaveholders of Scottish ancestry. Douglass and Garrison added their voices to the cries of local antislavery activists: "Send the money back." The church kept the money, but the dispute gained attention for Douglass's battle against American slavery.

Douglass's tour was not leisurely; during one busy month, he spoke almost every night. As usual, his blend of personal anecdotes and philosophical sermons was highly effective. For one speech, he read to the British a list of laws governing slaves in the American South: "If more than seven slaves together are found in any road without a white person, twenty lashes a piece; . . . for letting loose a boat from where it is made fast, thirty nine lashes for the first offense; and for the second shall have cut off from his head one ear; . . . for hunting with dogs in the woods, thirty lashes." He told his outraged audience that in the state of Virginia there were 71 crimes for which blacks could be executed, only 3 for whites.

In the same speech, Douglass declared, "It is necessary to resort to these cruelties in order to make a

According to Douglass, the temperance movement "has planted light and education where there was nothing but degredation, and darkness, and misery."

slave a slave, and to keep him a slave." He told how, when he was being beaten on Edward Covey's farm, all he had prayed for was that his life would be spared. "But," he continued, "as soon as the blow was not to be feared, then came the longing for liberty."

The World Temperance Convention that was held in London in August 1846 was the scene of Douglass's most controversial speech. There he attacked the American temperance movement because it failed to criticize slaveowners who used alcohol to pacify their work force. He also felt that the temperance activists were hostile to free blacks. The Reverend Samuel Cox, a member of the American delegation, publicly accused him of trying to destroy the unity of the temperance movement. Douglass responded that Cox was a bigot and, like many other clergymen, a secret supporter of slavery.

By the fall of 1846, Douglass's thoughts were turning toward home. Garrison and other friends convinced him to stay another six months, but Douglass rejected suggestions that he settle in England. In America his people labored in bondage. There was where his work lay. However, recapture remained a frightening possibility for Douglass if he returned to the United States. The problem was unexpectedly

Douglass said of the treatment of slaves, "To be accused was to be convicted, and to be convicted was to be punished."

resolved when two English friends of his raised enough money to buy his freedom. The required amount, $710.96, was sent to Hugh Auld, to whom Thomas Auld had transferred the title to Douglass. On December 5, 1846, Hugh Auld signed the papers that declared the 28-year-old Douglass a free man.

Douglass appreciated the gesture of his English friends, even though as an abolitionist he did not recognize Hugh Auld's right to own him. In his farewell speech to the British people, Douglass joked, "I have as much right to sell Hugh Auld as Hugh Auld had to sell me. If any of you are disposed to make a purchase of him, just say the word." Actually, Douglass said more seriously, he would not peddle human flesh.

In the spring of 1847, Douglass sailed from England, once again on board the *Cambria*. He had left the United States as a respected author and lecturer; he was returning with a huge international reputation. He had left as a fugitive slave; he was returning as his own master. Thousands of people had listened to his speeches, and he had aroused much goodwill for the abolitionist cause in the British Isles. His tour had been an unqualified success.

Douglass was met by happy friends and family upon his return home. However, some abolitionists criticized him for letting his freedom be bought because he was thereby acknowledging Hugh Auld's moral and legal right to own him. Douglass countered that his freedom was the gift of friends and that he recognized Hugh Auld as his kidnapper, not as his master. Now that the ransom had been paid, he could fight the battle against slavery with a free mind.

During his travels in England, Douglass had demonstrated some independence from the Garrisonian abolitionist faction, addressing a meeting sponsored by a rival antislavery group. Upon his return to America, he decided to found and edit a new abolitionist

The building in the center of this photograph shows a pen where slaves were kept when they were not working for a company based in Alexandria, Virginia.

newspaper with the help of funds raised by his English friends. Garrison opposed this plan, saying that there were already too many such journals and that Douglass was needed as a lecturer.

Douglass dropped the idea for a while. In August 1847, he joined Garrison on a lecture tour throughout the North, and the two abolitionists were greeted by thousands of admirers in many towns. Garrison became seriously ill, however, and Douglass was forced to continue the tour without him. After finishing the trip in the fall of 1847, he again began drawing up plans for a new abolitionist newspaper. The goal of his paper would be to trumpet the abolitionist cause and fight for black equality. Rather than publish his paper in New England, where the *Liberator* was based, Douglass decided to move farther west, to Rochester, New York. Anna and the children settled into a two-story brick house that Douglass bought there, and he went to work assembling printing materials.

On December 3, 1847, Douglass began his second career, when his four-page weekly newspaper, the

North Star, came off the presses. On the masthead appeared the motto, "Right is of no sex—Truth is of no color—God is the Father of us all, and we are all Brethren." Two other black abolitionists worked with Douglass on the *North Star* for a short while. The physician and future black nationalist leader Martin Delaney was an editor, and William Nell served as publisher. Douglass's children and two young apprentices helped to set the type used to print the paper.

Once the *North Star* began to circulate, Douglass's friends in the abolitionist movement rallied to join

Leaders of the women's rights movement Susan B. Anthony (left) and Elizabeth Cady Stanton gained the support of Douglass, who claimed in the motto of the North Star, "Right is of no sex."

in praising it. Garrison and others noted the high quality of the newspaper. However, not everyone was pleased to see another antislavery paper—especially one edited by an ex-slave. Some local citizens were unhappy that their town was the site of a black newspaper, and the *New York Herald* urged the citizens of Rochester to dump Douglass's printing press in Lake Ontario.

Gradually, Rochester came to take pride in the *North Star* and its bold editor. The town had a reputation for being strongly pro-abolitionist. Rochester's women were active in antislavery societies, and through them Douglass kept in close contact with the leaders in the fight for women's rights, among them Susan B. Anthony, Lucretia Mott, and Elizabeth Cady Stanton. Along with the good will of Rochester's abolitionists and female political activists, Douglass received encouragement from the local printers' union, whose members admired his work.

The *North Star* received a number of glowing reviews, but unfortunately the praises did not translate into financial success. The cost of producing a quality weekly was high, and subscriptions grew slowly. For a number of years, Douglass was forced to depend on his own savings and contributions from friends to keep the paper afloat. He returned to the lecture circuit to raise more money, and during the paper's first year, he was on the road for six months. In the spring of 1848, he even mortgaged his home.

In the midst of these troubles, a friend from England arrived to help Douglass with his financial problems. Julia Griffiths had raised funds to help launch the paper, and now she was prepared to fight for its survival. A good businesswoman, Griffiths put the *North Star*'s finances in order, and Douglass was eventually able to regain possession of his house. By 1851, he would be able to write to his friend, the abolitionist publisher and politician Gerrit Smith, "The *North*

Star sustains itself, and partly sustains my large family. It has reached a living point. Hitherto, the struggle of its life has been to live. Now it more than lives."

Despite many ups and downs, Douglass's newspaper would continue publication as a weekly until 1860 and would survive for three more years as a monthly. After 1851, it would be titled *Frederick Douglass' Paper*. For many people, Douglass's newspaper symbolized the potential for blacks to achieve whatever goals they set. It provided a forum for black writers and thinkers and highlighted the success achieved by prominent black figures in American society.

For Douglass, starting the *North Star* marked the end of his dependence on Garrison and other white abolitionists. The paper allowed him to discover in detail the problems facing blacks around the country. It also put him in contact with other black leaders, such as Henry Highland Garnet, a supporter of black emigration to Africa, and the abolitionist Charles Remond. Douglass had heated disputes with many of his fellow black activists, but these debates showed that his people were beginning to involve themselves in the center of events affecting their position in America.

Already an accomplished speaker, Douglass's work as an editor furthered his development as a writer, providing him, as he said, with "the best school possible." He honed his skills as week after week he wrote articles on important issues, an exercise that forced him to think and read and express his thoughts clearly.

By the end of the 1840s, Douglass was well on his way to becoming the most famous and respected black leader in the country. In great demand as a speaker and writer, he had proved himself to be an independent thinker and courageous spokesman for black liberty and equality. He had broken out of the bondage of his youth and had become a man. ◕

Henry Highland Garnet was a former slave who became a minister in New York City. Along with leading a black emigration movement, he called for slaves to put an end to their captivity by rebelling.

UNCLE TOM'S CABIN

UNCLE TOM & EVA.

5
THE GOSPEL OF STRUGGLE

DURING HIS YEARS in Rochester, Douglass continued to grow in stature as the editor of the nation's best-known black newspaper, in which he was free to attack slavery with all the power of his impressive intellect. Yet the approach of the tumultuous 1850s would severely test his faith in the ability of America to rid itself of the institution that kept his people in chains.

Some of the turmoil made its way into Douglass's home. While he roamed far beyond his original bounds, his wife, though hard-working, remained uneducated and politically unambitious. Even during their years in New Bedford, friends had worried that the couple's differences would put a strain on the marriage. In 1848, hoping to bridge the gap between them, Douglass hired a teacher for Anna. The effort failed, and Anna remained almost totally illiterate.

Douglass appreciated his wife's domestic skills, but he also admired the educated, politically active women who served in the antislavery and women's rights movements. He was grateful for all the help the women abolitionists had given blacks, and in 1848, he showed his support for the feminist cause by attending the first women's rights convention. The movement drew much hostile press, and the 35 women and 32 men who went to the convention were described as "man-

Harriet Beecher Stowe's Uncle Tom's Cabin *was one of the first American novels to depict the evils of slavery. Initially published in the early 1850s, it immediately became immensely popular.*

59

Feminist leader Lucretia Mott not only was instrumental in forming the first women's rights convention, but she also was involved in the abolitionist and temperance movements.

haters" and "hermaphrodites" (people with both male and female sexual features). The women delegates hesitated to make the demand for voting rights (suffrage) a part of their movement's platform, and the feminist leader Elizabeth Cady Stanton asked Douglass to speak on the matter. With an eloquent appeal for bold action, Douglass convinced the women that political equality was an essential step in their liberation.

The cause of women's rights would continue to remain close to Douglass's heart. Susan B. Anthony, Lucretia Mott, and many other feminists would be his lifelong friends. Perhaps it was inevitable that friendship between the handsome, articulate Douglass and one of the many women who admired him would erupt in scandal.

In 1848, Julia Griffiths began serving as Douglass's office and business manager and soon became his almost constant companion. She arranged his lectures, dealt with his paper's finances, and accompanied him to meetings. People in Rochester gradually adjusted to the sight of the black leader and the white woman strolling arm in arm down the street. But since Griffiths lived in the same house with Douglass and his wife, rumors began to fly.

Although Anna Douglass said little about the situation, she was plainly uneasy about the local talk. The controversy was even reported in the newspapers, and Douglass was attacked by the Garrisonians for involving the abolitionist movement in a scandal. In 1852, Griffiths decided to spare Douglass further embarrassment by moving out of the household. She remained his close associate until 1855, when she returned to England. The two continued to correspond with each other over the next 40 years.

Tensions between Douglass and William Lloyd Garrison had been growing even before the Griffiths controversy. After Douglass moved to Rochester and

started the *North Star*, he began to listen to abolitionists such as his friend Gerrit Smith, whose views
on how to fight slavery differed sharply from those of
Garrison. Gradually, Douglass's own beliefs began to
change.

The first of Garrison's principles that Douglass
began to question was the idea that resisting slavery
through violent means was wrong. In 1847, he met
with the militant white abolitionist John Brown, who
helped to convince Douglass that pacifist means, such
as moral persuasion, could not by themselves bring
an end to slavery. Brown told him that slaveholders
"had forfeited their right to live, and that slaves had
the right to gain their liberty in any way they could."
By 1849, Douglass himself was telling audiences at
abolitionist meetings that he would be pleased to hear
that the slaves in the South had revolted and "were
spreading death and destruction." Ten years later, he
had completely abandoned the idea that slavery could
be ended peacefully.

As Douglass widened his circle of abolitionist
friends, he also began to question Garrison's opposition to seeking antislavery reforms through the political process. In 1848, he urged women to fight for
the vote. How could he deny this counsel to his own
people? Garrison's view of the Constitution as a proslavery document was not accepted by all abolitionists, and as Douglass talked with these dissenters, he
began to see the matter in a different light. The
Constitution—with its emphasis on promoting the
general welfare and securing the blessings of liberty
for all—clearly seemed to be antislavery.

The North, Douglass realized, would never abolish slavery if that could only be done by dividing the
Union and dismantling the Constitution. He therefore decided that slavery would have to be ended
through political reforms. Through his association
with Gerrit Smith, who was one of the leaders of the

*Abolitionist John Brown (shown
here) believed that militant action
was the only way to end slavery.
Although Douglass did not agree
with all of Brown's methods, he
said of the activist, "The time is
coming when we shall be quite
ashamed of the reception given to
John Brown."*

Douglass encouraged meetings (such as the one shown here) to further women's rights. The first feminist convention took place in Seneca Falls, New York, in 1848.

antislavery Liberty party, Douglass began to become involved in politics. In 1848, he attended a convention of the Free Soil party, which was battling to stop the spread of slavery into the territories west of the Mississippi River.

The final split between Douglass and Garrison occurred at the annual meeting of the American Anti-Slavery Society in June 1851. There Douglass shocked his old associates by publicly announcing that he intended to urge the *North Star*'s readers to engage in politics. The Garrisonian press launched a vicious assault against him during the following months, and Douglass responded in kind. It would be many years before the breach between the two factions would heal.

The disputes between the antislavery factions did not dominate Douglass's life. He was active in any cause that furthered the progress of his people, and he attended many conventions of black abolitionists. At a meeting in 1853, he and other black leaders joined in demanding that blacks be given their full legal and political rights as American citizens. Douglass also tried to establish a black vocational school, an institution that would train its students to become skilled tradesmen. Among the people he visited in his efforts to raise funds for the school was Harriet Beecher Stowe, the author of the immensely popular antislavery novel *Uncle Tom's Cabin*. Unfortunately, Douglass was not able to collect enough money to start the school.

Although Douglass was often away from home, he was a proud and loving father. A fifth child, Annie, was born in 1849. Because Rochester's public schools refused to admit black students, Douglass at first enrolled his oldest child, Rosetta, in a private school. However, even there Rosetta was segregated from white pupils, and Douglass finally hired a woman to teach his children at home. The boys also worked in the *North Star*'s printing room. Never one to let racial discrimination go unchallenged, Douglass campaigned to end segregation in Rochester's school system, and in 1857 his efforts succeeded.

Events in Douglass's private life were overshadowed by Congress's struggle to decide how far slavery would be allowed to spread in the areas to the west of the Mississippi River. These territories—which would later become such states as Kansas and Ne-

Best known for the antislavery novel Uncle Tom's Cabin, *Harriet Beecher Stowe had no first-hand knowledge of what slavery was actually like in the South. She relied mostly on information supplied to her by a fugitive slave, Josiah Henson.*

An announcement in 1854 of a town meeting in Nebraska held to determine whether or not the territory should remain free or allow slavery. The decision was for slavery.

braska—were attracting many new settlers, some of whom favored slavery and some of whom opposed it. Congress was being pressed hard to maintain a balance between the interests of the southern slave states, which wanted no restrictions on slavery, and the northern free states, which wanted to reserve the western territories for free labor. Congressional measures had to be passed to ensure that there were equal numbers of free and slave states.

In 1820, Congress had passed the Missouri Compromise, establishing a line to the north of which no slavery would be allowed in the western territories. For every slave state that joined the Union, it was agreed that one free state would also be admitted. Thirty years later, however, northern and southern congressmen engaged in a bitter debate over California's application to enter the Union as a free state, which threatened to upset the critical balance. The passage of the Compromise of 1850 momentarily restored the peace and conferred statehood upon California, but it also introduced the Fugitive Slave Act, which put more teeth into previous laws requiring that runaway slaves be returned to their owners.

Tensions between Free Soil advocates and pro-slavery supporters remained high, but the Democrat-controlled Congress continued to push for compromise. In 1854, Congress passed the Kansas-Nebraska Act, which allowed slavery to extend its reach into the northern territories in the West. The act declared that the citizens of a new state would vote on whether they wanted slavery or not. Outraged by the Democrats' appeasement of southern slaveholders, some angry antislavery groups met to form the Republican party, which soon emerged as the second strongest party after the Democrats.

The new party took the lead in the moral crusade against slavery. But in 1857, the Supreme Court struck down almost all restrictions on slavery. In its infa-

Dred Scott was a slave who sued for his freedom after living for four years in a state where slavery was illegal. The Supreme Court ruled on his case in 1857, stating that slaves were not citizens of the United States and therefore "had no rights which the white man was bound to respect."

mous Dred Scott decision, the Court declared that slaves were property, just like a cow or a kettle; they could be taken by their masters into free states and remain legally bound to their owners. Chief Justice Roger Taney wrote that blacks "had no rights which the white man was bound to respect." The Court's shocking decision, which overturned the Missouri Compromise and the later congressional acts, gained the Republican party thousands of new supporters and led many northerners to actively defy the fugitive slave laws.

Douglass became deeply involved in helping runaway slaves (much like the ones shown here) escape to freedom after the passage of the Fugitive Slave Act in 1850.

After the passage of the Fugitive Slave Act in 1850, Douglass became strongly involved in the underground railroad, the system set up by antislavery groups to bring runaways to sanctuaries in the North and in Canada. "Passengers" on the underground railroad often began their journey from meeting points in the hills of western Virginia and other areas close to the North-South border. From there they were moved step by step through a network of safe "stations" run by brave "conductors." The fugitives were concealed in attics and barns along the escape route until transportation could be found to the next place of refuge. They often traveled on wagons, hidden in barrels or piles of hay. Even while journeying through free states, the runaways had to be on the lookout for slave catchers and federal law officers. In addition, the Fugitive Slave Act stated that all citizens must aid federal marshals in the capture of escaped slaves.

Special commissioners were appointed to help identify fugitives, and they received a larger fee if they decided that a prisoner was a runaway.

Douglass's home in Rochester was near the Canadian border, and during the 1850s it became an important station on the underground railroad. Eventually, he became the superintendent of the entire system in his area. He often found runaways sitting on the steps of his newspaper office when he arrived at work in the morning. At times, as many as 11 fugitives were hiding in his home. Over the years, he and Anna fed and sheltered hundreds of these exhausted men and women.

Only a few of the slaves who tried to escape from the South were successful. Douglas fiercely attacked the fugitive slave laws and the many atrocities that were being committed against runaway slaves. In a speech given in Rochester on Independence Day in

Slave revolts (such as the one shown in this illustration) were generally unsuccessful. According to an 1860 issue of the newspaper Douglass' Monthly, Douglass "was not advocating forcible emancipation, neither did he advocate any theory of peace which left the slaves helpless."

This illustration shows a blood-hound being trained to recognize the form of a slave. Bloodhounds were occasionally used to hunt down runaway slaves.

1852, Douglass pointed out how differently blacks and whites viewed the day's celebrations:

> What to the American slave is your Fourth of July? I answer, a day that reveals to him more than all the other days of the year, the gross injustice and cruelty to which he is the constant victim . . . To him your celebration is a sham . . . a thin veil to cover up crimes which would disgrace a nation of savages. There is not a nation of the earth guilty of practices more shocking and bloody than are the people of the United States.

The sufferings of the hunted fugitive slaves reminded Douglass that freedom for his oppressed people would never come easily. In a speech he made at a Canandaigua, New York, convention celebrating the 20th anniversary of the emancipation of slaves in the British West Indies, Douglass preached that blacks must unite to gain their liberty and that they must be prepared for a hard struggle. "If there is no struggle there is no progress," he said, characterizing those who chose to wait for freedom to be handed to them as men who "want rain without thunder and lightning, . . . the ocean without the awful roar of its many waters." Blacks, he said, would have to pay a heavy price to win their freedom. "We must do this by labor, by suffering, by sacrifice, and if needs be, by our lives and the lives of others."

While Douglass labored with his pen and with his voice, other men chose more violent ways to fight slavery. John Brown, the white antislavery fighter whom Douglass had first met in 1847, was one of these men. Brown dreamed of setting up armed camps in the Allegheny Mountains in Maryland, Virginia, and Pennsylvania. From these bases, Brown planned to lead raids on slave plantations and to send bands of freed slaves northward. Brown had introduced Douglass to militant abolitionism in 1847, and during the 1850s he was a frequent visitor to the Douglass home, where he entertained the children by using

John Brown climbs down the stairs on his way to the gallows after being found guilty of treason. His death on December 2, 1859, came shortly after he and his group of 18 men attacked the town of Harpers Ferry, Virginia, in an attempt to start a slave revolt.

Colonel Robert E. Lee (shown here) led the federal troops that captured John Brown and his men, who had stormed a United States armory at Harpers Ferry, Virginia. Lee later became the commanding general of the Confederate army.

their blocks to build models of the mountain bases he hoped to establish.

During the mid-1850s, Brown was the leader of one of the Free Soil bands fighting the proslavery forces in Kansas. But Brown wanted to start a slave insurrection in the South. In 1859, he decided to lead an attack on the northern Virginia town of Harpers Ferry, seize the weapons stored in the nearby federal armory, and hold the local citizens hostage while he rounded up slaves in the area. Gathering a small force of white and black volunteers, Brown rented a farm near Harpers Ferry and made his preparations.

From the farm, Brown wrote to Douglass, asking him to come to a meeting in Chambersburg, Pennsylvania, in August. There Brown spoke of his plans and urged Douglass to join in the attack. Douglass refused. He had agreed with Brown's earlier ideas, but he knew that an attack on federal property would enrage most Americans.

This was the last time Douglass and Brown met. On October 16, 1859, Brown and his men seized Harpers Ferry. The next night, federal troops led by Colonel Robert E. Lee marched into the town and stormed the armory where Brown's band was stationed. Brown was captured, and two of his sons were killed in the fighting. In less than two months, Brown was tried for treason, found guilty, and hanged.

Douglass was lecturing in Philadelphia when he received the news about Brown's raid, and he was warned that letters had been found that implicated him in the attack. The headlines for the newspapers' accounts of the incident featured his name prominently. Knowing that he stood little chance of a fair trial if he were captured and sent to Virginia, Douglass fled to Canada, narrowly avoiding federal officers seeking his arrest.

From his Canadian refuge, Douglass wrote letters in his own defense, justifying both his flight and his refusal to help Brown. One of the men captured during the raid said that Douglass had promised to appear at Harpers Ferry with reinforcements. Douglass denied this accusation, saying that he would never approve of attacks on federal property. But though he could not condone the raid, he praised Brown as a "noble old hero."

In November 1859, Douglass sailed to England to begin a lecture tour, a trip he had planned long before the incident at Harpers Ferry. As on his first visit, he was warmly received. The news of his near arrest only increased his popularity with his audiences, and his lectures helped to stir up more sympathy for the antislavery cause. In May 1860, just as he was about to continue his lecture tour in France, word reached him that his youngest child, Annie, had died. Heartbroken over the loss of the daughter whom he described as the "light and life of my house," Douglass decided to go home.

More than a half year had passed since the Harpers Ferry raid, and the public furor had already died. All charges against Douglass had been dropped. Brown had been executed, and he was already being lionized as a martyr for the abolitionist cause.

Glad to be back with his family again, Douglass knew that he was home—and home included not just Rochester but all of America, including the states in the South. It was a home filled with strife, but it was his, and he embraced it all: the land, the people, the Constitution, the Union. ✤

6
THE
WAR FOR
EMANCIPATION

———— •❦• ————

THE PRESIDENTIAL contest in 1860 featured many candidates. The Democrats had split into factions; those who were proslavery supported Vicepresident John Breckinridge, while moderates in the North favored the Illinois senator Stephen Douglas. Abraham Lincoln was the candidate of the Republicans, who were opposed to the spread of slavery into new territories. The candidate from the newly formed Constitutional Union party was fighting to preserve national unity at any cost, and Gerrit Smith, Douglass's close friend, was running on a strong antislavery platform.

At first, Douglass campaigned for Smith, a wealthy abolitionist who had given financial support to John Brown and had backed Douglass's newspaper. However, a few months before the election, Douglass decided that Smith had no chance of winning and chose instead to back Lincoln. The Republican candidate's antislavery sentiments were well known, although he did not take as strong a position on emancipation as Douglass would have hoped.

The two Democratic candidates together received far more votes than anyone else did, but the division in the party gave the presidency to Lincoln. Unwilling to accept the results of the election, South Carolina seceded from the Union in late December

The inauguration of Mississippi senator Jefferson Davis as president of the Confederate States of America took place on February 18, 1861, at the State Capitol in Montgomery, Alabama.

Illinois senator Stephen Douglas (pictured on the balcony) of the Democratic party was Republican candidate Abraham Lincoln's chief rival for the presidency in 1860. This satirical drawing is from a Republican campaign newspaper.

1860. Abolitionists became the targets of angry mobs in the North, which blamed them for dividing the nation. At a meeting in Boston, Douglass was thrown down a staircase.

Northern attempts to win back the South were of little use, however. In February 1861, six more southern states—Georgia, Florida, Mississippi, Alabama, Louisiana, and Texas—seceded and established a separate government under the name of the Confederate States of America. Mississippi senator Jefferson Davis was elected as their president.

The country waited for Lincoln to respond to the crisis. The president's inaugural address in March was a disappointment to Douglass. Lincoln promised to uphold the fugitive slave laws and not to interfere with slavery in the states where it was already established. His first priority was to restore the Union, not to end slavery.

Despairing of any hope that slavery could be ended, Douglass began to consider the possibility of organizing a black emigration to the Caribbean nation of Haiti. In 1801, a rebellion led by the great liberation fighter Toussaint L'Ouverture had defeated the French rulers on the island and resulted in the establishment of the first black republic in 1804. Believing that Haiti might serve as a good home for black Americans, Douglass made plans to sail to the island and investigate conditions there.

On April 12, 1861, Confederate troops bombarded Fort Sumter, a federal installation in the harbor of Charleston, South Carolina. The fort surrendered a day later. Lincoln called for 75,000 troops to be mustered to put down the rebellion in the South. Virginia, Tennessee, North Carolina, and Arkansas immediately joined the Confederacy. The four other slave states—Delaware, Maryland, Missouri, and Kentucky—remained in the Union, although many soldiers from these so-called border states joined the Confederate army.

The two sides prepared for battle, the North with its 23 states and population of 22 million against the South's 11 states and 9 million people, including 3 and a half million slaves. The North was fighting to preserve the Union; the South was fighting for the right to secede and establish a nation that guaranteed a person's right to own slaves.

For Frederick Douglass and the abolitionists, the war was a battle to end slavery. Douglass's response to the surrender of Fort Sumter was one of thanksgiving. His prophecy was coming true: the nation must abolish slavery or be abolished by it. As the Civil War got under way, Douglass marked out two goals for which he would fight: emancipation for all slaves in the Confederacy and the Union border states, and the right of blacks to enlist in the armies of the North. As the war progressed, more and more people in the North would come to agree with these aims.

While battles raged throughout the South, Douglass traveled on the lecture circuit, calling for Lincoln to grant slaves their freedom. The president's actions early in the war were a blow to Douglass. When General John C. Frémont liberated all the slaves of Confederate sympathizers in Missouri, Lincoln revoked the order. He also overruled General David Hunter when the officer freed blacks captured from slaveowners in South Carolina, Georgia, and Florida. On April 16, 1862, the president signed a bill outlawing slavery in Washington, D.C., but he was slow to approve congressional measures confiscating slaves in captured areas of the South. Lincoln believed that if he passed laws that emancipated the slaves, the Union's border states might rebel and join the Confederacy.

Douglass continued to insist in his speeches and newspaper editorials that the aim of the war must be

Although Jefferson Davis was anxious to preserve the Union, his support of states' rights caused him to side with the South during the Civil War.

President Abraham Lincoln (holding a sheet of paper) discusses the Emancipation Proclamation with his cabinet. Issued just before the start of 1863, the proclamation freed millions of slaves from bondage.

to abolish slavery and that blacks must be allowed to join in the battle for their freedom. By refusing to let blacks fight in the Union armies, the North was depriving itself of thousands of willing and able soldiers. Battlefield casualties were frighteningly high, and antidraft riots erupted in northern cities. Blacks were frequently made the scapegoats of mobs demanding an end to the war. Meanwhile, the South's armies conscripted slaves to dig trenches and do other heavy labor. Gradually, as the costly war dragged on, with no final victory in sight for the North, Lincoln began to realize that stronger actions needed to be taken against the rebellious Confederacy.

In the summer of 1862, Lincoln read to his cabinet a draft of an order that would emancipate slaves in the Confederate states. He decided to issue the proclamation as soon as the North won a major battle. In September, Lincoln got his victory when northern troops pushed back a Confederate army at the bloody battle of Antietam in Maryland. On the night of December 31, 1862, the president issued the Emancipation Proclamation, declaring that as of the next day all slaves in areas not held by Union troops were free. Slavery was not abolished in the border states or in already captured areas of the South. Nevertheless, Lincoln's act freed millions of blacks, who fled from their masters and took "freedom's road" to areas controlled by Union forces.

In Boston on the night that the proclamation was announced, Douglass wrote of the spirit of those who had gathered with him at the telegraph office to witness slavery's death throes: "We were waiting and listening as for a bolt from the sky . . . we were watching . . . by the dim light of the stars for the dawn of a new day . . . we were longing for the answer to the agonizing prayers of centuries." The jubilant crowds cheered. The end of slavery was in sight.

Douglass next turned his attention to the struggle of blacks to be allowed to fight for their freedom. Early in 1863, Congress authorized black enlistment in the Union army. The Massachusetts 54th Regi-

This illustration shows slaves fleeing from their masters following the announcement of the Emancipation Proclamation.

ment was the first black unit to be formed, and the governor of the state asked Douglass to assist in recruitment. Douglass agreed and wrote a passionate editorial that was printed in the local newspapers. In "Men of Color, to Arms," he urged blacks to "end in a day the bondage of centuries" and to earn their equality and show their patriotism by fighting in the Union cause. His sons Lewis and Charles were among the first to enlist.

Unfortunately, Douglass's recruitment speeches promised black soldiers an equality they did not get in the Union army. They were paid one half of what white soldiers received and were given inferior weapons and inadequate training. Blacks were not allowed to become officers. Worst of all, black soldiers who were captured by Confederate troops were often shot.

When Douglass learned about these conditions, he halted his recruitment efforts. After publishing his complaints, he asked for an interview with the president, a request that was granted in the summer of 1863. Despite his political differences with the pres-

News of the Emancipation Proclamation reaches the South, informing slaves of their freedom.

ident, Douglass was immediately impressed by the warmth of Lincoln's personality. "I at once felt myself in the presence of an honest man," Douglass wrote, "one whom I could love, honor, and trust without reserve or doubt."

Douglass explained to the president his concerns about the way black soldiers were being treated by Union officers and Confederate captors. Douglass wrote that Lincoln's response was "serious and even troubled." The president did not promise to resolve all of the problems, but he gave Douglass some encouragement that changes might be made in the future. Although not entirely satisfied with Lincoln's answer, Douglass decided to begin recruiting again.

Shortly after the meeting, Secretary of War Edwin Stanton offered Douglass a commission on the staff of General Lorenzo Thomas. Douglass accepted the offer and returned to Rochester, where he published the last issue of his newspaper. He waited at home for notice of his commission as an officer, but it never arrived. Apparently, Stanton decided that Douglass would never be accepted by other officers.

Douglass was extremely disappointed that the commission fell through, but he continued his recruiting work. By now, Frederick, Jr., had joined his brothers in the Union lines. More than 200,000 blacks enlisted in the Union army and 38,000 were killed or wounded in Civil War battles. Comprising about 10 percent of the North's troops, the black soldiers made their numbers felt on the battlefields and distinguished themselves in many engagements. By mid-1864, with the help of the spirited black troops, the war was slowly turning in favor of the North. The South was becoming increasingly isolated as Britain and other European nations gave their endorsement to the North's battle to end slavery.

By 1864, Douglass was becoming concerned about what the fate of blacks in America would be once

Black enlistment in the Union army was authorized by Congress in early 1863. Douglass assisted in the recruitment of the first black regiment by writing a widely published newspaper editorial, "Men of Color, to Arms."

they were all free. Lincoln seemed uninterested in the question of voting rights for blacks, and discrimination against black soldiers and civilians in the North continued. Douglass could not be satisfied with the liberation of the slaves alone; he wanted equality for his people. Like many other abolitionists, he did not believe that Lincoln had a strong enough commitment to improving conditions for blacks.

In May 1864, with the presidential elections approaching, Douglass attended a convention of abolitionists and zealous antislavery members of the Republican party, who were known as radical Republicans. The delegates nominated the former Free Soil party candidate and Union general John C. Frémont for president. The Democrats selected the popular general George McClellan to run against Lincoln on a Copperhead platform. Copperhead was the derogatory name used to refer to anyone who favored making immediate peace with the South and leaving slaves in bondage. Worried that McClellan might win the election, Douglass and other Frémont supporters decided to back Lincoln.

Douglass and Lincoln had a second meeting in August 1864. The weary president had begun to doubt that the war could be won, and he was worried that he might have to sign a peace with the Confederacy

Despite Douglass's assurances during his recruitment of black soldiers that they would be treated on a par with whites, black troops continually faced discrimination by the Union army as well as by the federal government.

that would leave slavery intact. Lincoln asked Douglass to draw up plans for leading slaves out of the South in the event that a Union victory seemed impossible. Douglass left the interview convinced that the humane president was a friend of blacks. He was also aware that Lincoln walked a lonely road. The president's policies were hated not only by the South but by many people in the North who had grown tired of war.

The evacuation plan that Douglass sent to Lincoln never had to be used. In the summer of 1864, General William T. Sherman and his Union troops left a path of destruction as they marched through the heart of the South. In September, Sherman entered Atlanta, the capital of Georgia, and then pressed on to Savannah, with his troops singing refrains from a popular war song, "John Brown's body lies a-moldering in the grave; His soul is marching on." The victories gave the North renewed heart and helped Lincoln win easy reelection in November.

The dreams of the Confederacy died hard. By the end of 1864, the South was hungry and bankrupt. As the ragtag Confederate armies retreated before their better-supplied opponents, Douglass took the occasion to visit Maryland and Union-controlled areas of Virginia. He lectured in his old home town of

Union general William Sherman sought to end the Civil War by wiping out the productive capabilities of the South—and destroying Confederate morale in the process.

President Abraham Lincoln rode through the Confederate capital of Richmond, Virginia, on April 4, 1864, shortly after the city was captured by Union troops.

Baltimore, where once he had toiled as a slave. Now he spoke as a free man—and an eminently successful one. On this trip, he was reunited with his sister Eliza, whom he had not seen in 30 years. He was very proud of his sister, who through her own hard work had managed to buy the freedom of herself and her nine children.

Back in the North, Douglass attended Lincoln's second inaugural address. Standing among the crowds gathered in the nation's capital, Douglass felt himself to be "a man among men." As though to prick that bubble, government officials refused to allow Douglass or any other black to attend the evening reception in the White House. But when Douglass sent word of this refusal to the president, he was quickly ushered in to the ceremony. Lincoln personally greeted him with the words, "Here comes my friend Douglass." This was indeed the man of whom Douglass would write, "In his company, I was never in any way reminded of my humble origins or of my unpopular color."

The assassination of President Abraham Lincoln by John Wilkes Booth took place on April 14, 1865, at Ford's Theater in Washington, D.C. Douglass was among those who gave a eulogy for the slain leader.

In the beginning of April, the Confederate capital of Richmond, Virginia, was captured. Lincoln himself rode through the devastated city and heard himself called "Messiah" by rejoicing blacks. A few days later, the commander of the Confederate forces, General Robert E. Lee, surrendered to the Union commander, Ulysses S. Grant, at Appomattox Court House in Virginia. On April 9, 1865, the Civil War was over.

To the horror of the newly reunited nation, President Lincoln was assassinated by a proslavery fanatic, John Wilkes Booth, while attending a play at Ford's Theater in Washington on April 14. He died the next day. With the rest of the country, Douglass mourned the man he had grown to respect.

No sadness could completely overshadow Douglass's joy at this time, however. A single, glorious fact remained: the war to end slavery had been won. All his life's work had led to this moment. Now it was here. ✺

7

"THE WORK BEFORE US"

◄◑►

WITH THE RATIFICATION of the Thirteenth Amendment to the U.S. Constitution in December 1865, slavery was officially abolished in all areas of the United States. The Reconstruction era was under way in the South, the period during which the 11 Confederate states would be gradually reintroduced to the Union. In the meantime, Northern armies continued to occupy the South and to enforce the decrees of Congress.

Frederick Douglass was then 47 years old, an active man in the prime of his life. No longer enlisted in the war on slavery, he thought about buying a farm and settling down to a quiet life. But black Americans still desperately needed a champion, and Douglass soon rejected any notion of an early retirement.

In many parts of the South, the newly freed slaves labored under conditions similar to those existing before the war. The Union army could offer only limited protection to the ex-slaves, and Lincoln's successor, Andrew Johnson of Tennessee, clearly had no interest in ensuring the freedom of southern blacks. The new president's appointments as governors of southern states formed conservative, proslavery governments. The new state legislatures passed laws de-

Although the Thirteenth Amendment officially abolished slavery in the United States in 1865, blacks (such as the ones shown here) continued to be severely mistreated in the South.

85

President Andrew Johnson vetoed
the Freedman's Bureau Bill,
which sought to provide assistance
to blacks throughout the South.
Congress passed the bill over his
veto on July 16, 1866.

signed to keep blacks in poverty and in positions of servitude. Under these so-called black codes, ex-slaves who had no steady employment could be arrested and ordered to pay stiff fines. Prisoners who could not pay the sum were hired out as virtual slaves. In some areas, black children could be forced to serve as apprentices in local industries. Blacks were also prevented from buying land and were denied fair wages for their work.

Despite the fact that blacks were being so poorly treated in the South, some abolitionists believed that their work was done. At a meeting of the American Anti-Slavery Society in May 1865, one month after the end of the Civil War, William Lloyd Garrison had called upon the organization to disband, now that its goal was accomplished. Douglass came out against Garrison's proposal, stating that "Slavery is not abolished until the black man has the ballot." The society voted to continue the struggle for black rights, but many abolitionists left the movement.

Fortunately, abolitionists were not the only ones interested in giving blacks the right to vote. The Republican party was worried that the Democrats would regain their power in the South. If this happened, the Republicans would lose their dominant position in Congress when the southern states were readmitted to the Union. Led by two fierce antislavery senators, Thaddeus Stevens and Charles Sumner, a group of radical Republicans joined with abolitionists in a campaign for voting rights for black men, who, they believed, would naturally support the Republicans.

During the later part of 1865, Douglass traveled throughout the North, speaking out for black suffrage and warning the country that the former slaveholders were regaining control of the South. In February 1866, he addressed his most important audience, President Andrew Johnson. Along with his son Lewis and three other black leaders, Douglass met with Johnson to impress upon him the need for changes in the southern state governments. The president did most of the talking, and he told the delegation that he intended to support the interests of southern whites and to block voting rights for blacks. Douglass and Johnson parted, both saying that they would take their cases to the American people.

Despite the president's opposition, Douglass and the supporters continued to battle for black rights with some success. The public mood gradually turned against Johnson and his attempts to install governments in the South that were controlled by Confederate loyalists. The Republican-controlled Congress became increasingly resistant to Johnson's plans for a limited reconstruction of the the southern states. The radical Republicans wanted to see sweeping changes enforced that would end the former slaveholders' power in the South. Thaddeus Stevens urged that the estates of the large slaveholders be broken up and the land distributed to ex-slaves, or freedmen, as they were then known.

The Freedman's Bureau was established by the federal government to provide all forms of relief to poor blacks throughout the South.

VOTE FOR HAYES!   SOUTHERN LIBERTY.

                                                   ACK SUPREMA

Although the ratification of the Fourteenth Amendment in July 1868 granted full citizenship to blacks, several states continued to deprive them of the right to vote.

In the summer of 1866, Congress passed two bills over the president's veto. One, the Freedmen's Bureau Bill, extended the powers of a government agency that had been established in 1865 for the purpose of providing medical, educational, and financial assistance for the millions of impoverished southern blacks. Congress also passed the Civil Rights Bill, which gave full citizenship to blacks, along with all the rights enjoyed by other Americans.

President Johnson's supporters, mainly Democrats and conservative Republicans, organized in the summer of 1866 to stop the movement for further black rights. The radical Republicans also held a meeting in Philadelphia to vote on a resolution calling for black suffrage, and Douglass attended the convention as a delegate from New York. Unfortunately, he encountered much prejudice from some Republican politicians, who were unwilling to associate with blacks on an equal level. Nonetheless, Douglass went to the convention and spoke out for black suffrage. The vote on the resolution was a close one, for some of the delegates were afraid that white voters would not support a party that allied itself too closely with blacks.

Speeches by Douglass and the woman suffragist Anna E. Dickinson helped turn the tide in favor of black suffrage.

For Douglass, the convention also held a more personal note. While marching in a parade of delegates, he spotted Amanda Sears, whose mother, Lucretia Auld, had given him his first pair of pants and arranged for him to leave the Lloyd plantation. Sears and her two children had traveled to Philadelphia just to see the famed Frederick Douglass.

The movement for black suffrage grew rapidly after the Philadelphia convention. With President Johnson's supporters greatly outnumbered, in June 1866, Congress passed the Fourteenth Amendment, which was designed to ensure that rights guaranteed earlier to blacks under the Civil Rights Bill were protected by the Constitution. The amendment was finally ratified in July 1868 after all the states approved it. Although the new amendment declared that no state could deny any person his full rights as an American citizen, it did not guarantee blacks the right to vote. In most states, however, blacks were already voting.

During July 1867, Douglass was asked by President Johnson to take charge of the Freedman's Bureau, a position that would have allowed him to oversee all the government programs administering to the needs of southern blacks. Douglass was tempted by the offer— the first major post to be offered to a black man— but he realized that by associating with the Johnson administration, he would be helping the president appear to be the black man's friend. Instead, he refused to serve under a man whose policies he detested.

By 1867, Douglass could see that Johnson's days in office were numbered. The president was unable to stop Congress's Reconstruction acts, which divided the South into five military districts and laid out strict guidelines for the readmission of the Confederate states

During the Reconstruction era, schools were established to teach former slaves how to read and write.

Commander in chief of the Union army during the Civil War, Ulysses S. Grant (shown here) was supported by Douglass in his bid to become president of the United States in 1868.

into the Union. The new laws required the southern states to ratify the Fourteenth Amendment and to guarantee blacks the right to vote. The radical Republicans were angered by Johnson's attempts to block the Reconstruction measures, and they instituted impeachment proceedings against him, the first time a president underwent this ordeal. The impeachment measure fell one vote short of the two-thirds majority in the House and Senate needed to remove Johnson from office, but the president exercised little power during the last two years of his term.

During the 1868 presidential contest, Douglass campaigned for the Republican candidate, Ulysses S. Grant, the former commander in chief of the Union army. In a famous speech, "The Work Before Us," Douglass attacked the Democratic party for ignoring black citizens and warned about the rise in the South of white supremacist organizations such as the Ku Klux Klan. These secret societies attempted to intimidate blacks with fire and the hangman's noose. They also attacked "Yankee carpetbaggers" (northerners who had flooded into the South at the end of the Civil War) and "scalawags" (southern whites who cooperated with the federal Reconstruction authorities).

Douglass feared that the terrorist tactics of the Klan would succeed in frightening blacks into giving up the civil rights they had gained in the South. "Rebellion has been subdued, slavery abolished, and peace proclaimed," he said, "and yet our work is not done. . . . We are face to face with the same old enemy of liberty and progress. . . . The South today is a field of blood."

Black voters came out strongly for the Republicans in the 1868 elections, helping Grant win the presidency. With Grant in office, the Fifteenth Amendment passed through Congress and was submitted to the states for ratification. This amendment guaranteed all citizens the right to vote, regardless of their race. Douglass's push for state approval of the amendment caused a breach between him and the woman suffragists, who were upset that the measure did not include voting rights for woman. Old friends such as Susan B. Anthony and Elizabeth Cady Stanton accused Douglass of abandoning the cause of women's rights.

At the annual meeting of the Equal Rights Association in May 1869, Douglass tried to persuade the woman suffragists that voting rights for blacks must be won immediately, while women could afford to wait. "When women because they are women are dragged from their homes and hung upon lamp-posts, . . . then they will have the urgency to obtain the ballot," said Douglass. One of the women in the crowd cried out, "Is that not also true about black women?" "Yes, yes," Douglass replied, "but not because she is a woman but because she is black." The women in the audience were not convinced by Douglass's argument, and some of them even spoke out against black suffrage. Douglass's relationship with the woman suffragists eventually healed, but women would not receive the right to vote until 1920.

The campaign for state ratification of the Fifteenth Amendment was successful. On March 30,

This illustration depicts the widespread belief among white Southerners during the Reconstruction era that education and voting privileges for blacks made them dangerous.

The ratification of the Fifteenth Amendment to the Constitution in 1870 guaranteed the right to vote to all citizens of the United States—including former slaves. Women would not be given the ballot until 1920.

1870, President Grant declared that the amendment had been adopted. Later, at the last official meeting of the American Anti-Slavery Society, Douglass spoke gratefully about the new rights blacks had won. "I seem to be living in a new world," he said. While thanking all the men and women who had struggled for so long to make this new world possible, he modestly omitted his own name.

However, no one had fought harder for black rights than Douglass. By 1870, he could look proudly upon some of the fruits of his labors. Between 1868 and 1870, the southern states were readmitted to the Union, and large numbers of blacks were elected to the state legislatures. Blacks also won seats in Congress, with Hiram Revels of Mississippi becoming the first black senator and Joseph Rainey of South Carolina being the first black to enter the House of Representatives.

In 1870, Douglass was asked to serve as editor of a newspaper based in Washington, D.C., whose goal was to herald the progress of blacks throughout the country. Early on, the paper, the *New National Era*, experienced financial difficulties, and Douglass bought the enterprise. The paper folded in 1874, but for a few years it provided him with the means to publish his opinions on the developing racial situation in the United States.

Another misfortune occurred in 1872, when Douglass's Rochester home went up in flames. None of his family was hurt, but many irreplaceable volumes of his newspapers were destroyed. Although friends urged him to rebuild in Rochester, Douglass decided to move his family to the center of political activity in Washington, D.C.

During 1872, Douglass campaigned hard for the reelection of President Grant. He supported the president even though many of the Republican party leaders he most respected, including Senator Charles Sumner, chose to back the Democratic candidate, Horace Greeley. Although personally honest, Grant was harshly criticized for not controlling the corrupt officials who served in his administration. Douglass stuck with the president, believing that blacks needed a strong friend in the White House. At the time, the Ku Klux Klan and other white terrorist organizations were burning black schools and murdering school-teachers in an effort to keep southern blacks from learning how to read.

Grant easily won the 1872 election, and Douglass was given an unexpected honor. He was chosen as one of the two electors-at-large from New York, the men who carried the sealed envelope with the results of the state voting to the capital. After the election, Douglass expected that he would be given a position in the Grant administration, but no post was offered, so he returned to the lecture circuit.

"I have sometimes thought that the American people are too great to be small, too just and magnan-imous to oppress the weak," Douglass said. However, racial oppression often left him with doubts about his countrymen.

A third financial loss struck Douglass in 1874. That year he was offered and accepted the position of president of the Freedmen's Savings and Trust Company, a bank that had been founded to encourage blacks to invest and save their money. The previous management had made huge loans to speculators at extremely low interest rates, however. By the time Douglass was put in charge, the bank was on the verge of collapse. He immediately appealed to Congress for help and tried to restore confidence by investing much of his own money in the bank. Even so, the prestigious Freedmen's Bank failed, and many black depositors lost their money. For Douglass, it was a blow to his pride as well as to his pocketbook.

Fortunately, Douglass had the means to recoup his losses on the lecture circuit. He no longer spoke simply about black rights but included other topics

The failure of the Freedmen's Savings and Trust Company proved to be a great financial blow to Douglass, the bank's president, as well as to other black investors.

on which he was an authority, such as Scandinavian folklore. On whatever subject he lectured, he combined his humor, intelligence, and passion to create a memorable experience for his listeners. Many people described him as one of the world's greatest speakers.

As Douglass traveled, he continued the battle against the daily humiliations that blacks were forced to endure throughout the country. Whenever he encountered discriminatory practices in a restaurant, hotel, or railway car, he would write a letter of protest to the local newspapers. In such ways, he retained his position as the foremost spokesman for black Americans. In 1875, he was cheered by Congress's passage of the Civil Rights Bill, which gave blacks the right to equal treatment in theaters, inns, and other public places.

In 1877, after the inauguration of the new Republican president, Rutherford B. Hayes, Douglass was finally rewarded with a political post, the largely ceremonial position of marshal for Washington, D.C. However, in order to court southern votes for the close presidential election of 1876, the Republicans had agreed to remove the bulk of the federal troops in the South. The rights that had been granted to blacks after the Civil War could no longer be protected in the southern states. Douglass was criticized for accepting his post after the Republicans' betrayal of their black supporters, but he saw the appointment as simply another milestone for his people. In any case, Douglass did speak out against the Republicans for abandoning southern blacks to the terror of white mobs.

Nearing the age of 60, Douglass was ready to give up his life on the road. In his undemanding job as a U.S. marshal overseeing the criminal justice system in the nation's capital, he was aided by a large staff

President Rutherford Hayes (shown here) appointed Douglass to the post of United States marshal for the District of Columbia in 1877.

In the late 1870s, Douglass and his family moved into this house at Cedar Hill, in the area of Washington, D.C.

of employees. Following his appointment, he purchased a new home in the Washington area. The 15-acre estate that he christened Cedar Hill included a 20-room house, which held a huge library and whose walls were decorated with the portraits of Abraham Lincoln, William Lloyd Garrison, Susan B. Anthony, and other people who had influenced him. His children were frequent visitors to Cedar Hill, and he greatly enjoyed playing the role of family patriarch.

In 1877, Douglass traveled to St. Michaels, Maryland, to visit old friends and to see the farms and plantations where he had worked as a slave. While there, he took the opportunity to visit his old master, Thomas Auld. Aged and feeble, Auld greeted his former slave as Marshal Douglass, and the two men spoke for a long time. Auld both justified and apologized for his actions as a slaveholder. Overall, the former master and slave were able to part on good terms.

After the 1880 election of the Republican candidate James Garfield as president, Douglass was appointed to the post of recorder of deeds for Washington, D.C. He liked his new job, which entailed managing the department that made records of property sales in the capital. During his five years in this position, he had ample time for his writing projects and speaking engagements. In 1881, he published the third of his autobiographical volumes, *Life and Times of Frederick Douglass*.

In August 1882, Anna Douglass died after a long illness. Douglass observed a traditional year of grieving, but he was hardly ready to settle into the life of a widower. He had never shrunk from controversy, and his next act upset both black and white society. In early 1884, Douglass announced that he was marrying Helen Pitts, a white woman who was nearly 20 years younger than he was. ◑

President James Garfield (shown here) appointed Douglass to the post of recorder of deeds for Washington, D.C., in 1880.

8

INDIAN
SUMMER

❦

DOUGLASS'S SECOND MARRIAGE in January 1884 aroused a storm of criticism. Many whites were outraged at his impudence in marrying outside his race, and some congressmen called for a ban on interracial marriages in the nation's capital. Blacks felt that he was showing contempt for his race. In addition, his children never fully accepted their father's new wife, and Helen's father refused to forgive his daughter for marrying a black man.

Born of a white father and black mother, Douglass did not see anything in his second marriage that was inconsistent with his beliefs. His goal had never been a world in which black and white were separated. He believed that all people deserved justice and freedom and certain human rights, among which was the right to follow one's own choice in love and marriage.

A native of Rochester, Helen Pitts Douglass was an educated woman who had worked as a secretary at the recorder of deeds office. Tall and gracious, she was complimented by one writer as a woman who "shows the subordination of a younger person to her husband." Douglass, however, felt that in Helen he had found an equal. When asked to attend a woman suffrage convention, he wrote back that Helen would be accompanying him for "she is not less a woman suffragist than myself." The marriage brought great

Douglass with his wife, Helen (seated), and their niece Eva Pitts.

Democratic president Grover Cleveland (shown here) asked Douglass to resign from his office as the recorder of deeds because he was a member of the Republican party.

happiness to both of them. A number of visitors to Cedar Hill commented on the radiance that seemed to surround the couple. "Love came to me," Helen said, "and I was not afraid to marry the man I loved because of his color."

Gradually, the controversy subsided, and Douglass was able to bask in the warmth of the Indian summer of his life. In 1884 a Democrat, Grover Cleveland, was elected president, and Douglass resigned his post as recorder of deeds shortly thereafter. In a late but glorious honeymoon, he and his wife sailed for Europe in mid-1886. While in England, Douglass visited Julia Griffiths as well as the two women who had purchased his freedom nearly 40 years before. The Douglasses then traveled to France, Italy, Egypt, and Greece. Discovering new lands at the age of 68, Douglass again felt young at heart.

In 1888, Douglass made a tour of the Deep South. Seeing the shacks that poor black tenant farmers lived in, he realized that he had grown out of touch with the conditions experienced by the majority of his people. Many lived in virtual slavery. In Washington, D.C., for the 26th anniversary of the Emancipation Proclamation, Douglass spoke with rage about how blacks were being exploited and were being denied their civil rights. Five years before, when the Supreme Court had struck down the Civil Rights Act of 1875 on the grounds that discrimination practiced by individuals was legal, Douglass had bitterly protested that the 14th and 15th Amendments were being undermined. Now he returned to this theme.

Such speeches helped to redeem Douglass's reputation among his critics in the black community. Some people thought he had grown too close to the Washington political establishment and had distanced himself from the masses of impoverished black laborers. On occasion, Douglass's ties to the Republican party may have led him to make compromises, but he always spoke out forcefully against racial injustice.

In 1889, a Republican president, Benjamin Harrison, replaced Grover Cleveland in office. Harrison offered Douglass an appointment as the American consul-general to Haiti. His friends urged him not to take the post, saying that it was too minor for him and that the humid Haitian climate would be bad for his health. Nevertheless, he believed it an honor to serve as his country's chief representative to the world's oldest black republic, and he accepted the offer.

Douglass and the Haitians got along very well. They were proud to be dealing with the famous champion of black rights, and he was careful to treat the small republic with the utmost respect. Unfortunately, Douglass became embroiled in the attempts of the U.S. government to establish a naval base on Haiti. He was also asked to help win concessions for

In "The Lesson of the Hour; Why the Negro is Lynched," Douglass wrote that mob violence against blacks was not the work of ignorant men alone. He maintained that "the upper classes of the South seem to be in full sympathy" with such acts because they kept blacks under control.

Douglass said of the violence that continued to plague blacks, "Some men have even shown an interest in saving my soul; but of what avail are such manifestations where one sees himself ostracized, degraded and denied the means of obtaining his daily bread?"

American businesses. Although he believed that the United States had much to offer the impoverished Caribbean nation, he opposed the heavy-handed negotiating tactics used by his government. He knew how much the Haitians feared American domination, and they eventually did turn down the U.S. requests. Because Douglass refused to exert diplomatic pressure on the Haitian government, the American press blamed him for the failure to win the naval base.

By 1891, Douglass's health had begun to suffer, and he decided to resign the consulship and return to the United States. The Haitians were sorry to see him go. In 1893, as a measure of its repect for him, the Haitian government asked him to be its representative to the World's Columbian Exposition, the international fair held in Chicago. Douglass was the only black American to play an official role at the exposition, and he wrote and published a pamphlet protesting that his country was ignoring its black citizens and denying them their civil rights.

After his return to the United States, Douglass resumed his quiet life at Cedar Hill. Rising at dawn to take his stroll around the estate's grounds, he spent his mornings and afternoons writing. In the evenings he played the violin while Helen accompanied him on the piano. He also continued with his speaking engagements.

Throughout his years as a lecturer, Douglass had constantly emphasized the need for blacks to rebel against any form of racial discrimination. He also told his people that they must take advantage of educational opportunities and work hard to build a prominent place for themselves in America. To succeed, blacks had to maintain their self-respect in the face of prejudice and oppression. Douglass's speeches would strongly influence the black leaders who would follow him: Booker T. Washington, Ida Wells-Barnett, Mary Church Terrell, W. E. B. Du Bois, and many others.

Throughout his life, Douglass proved to be an extremely prolific writer. He is shown here in his study at Cedar Hill.

In his final years, Douglass devoted much of his energies to speaking out against the country's lack of concern about the lynching of blacks in the South. Almost daily in the 1890s, new accounts were heard of black men being accused of raping a white woman and then being seized by a mob and hanged or burned to death. The crime of rape was almost never proved, but it was a charge that was sure to inflame the prejudices of white Americans and make them willing to condone the violent acts that were carried out against blacks.

Douglass made a thorough examination of the lynching issue in his essay, "The Lesson of the Hour; Why the Negro is Lynched." He placed much of the blame for the racial violence on the wealthy southern elite, which encouraged bigoted whites to "keep the Negros in their place." Once again, he denounced the schemes proposed by leaders of both races to deport blacks from the United States and colonize them in Africa and other foreign lands. "We are here and are here to stay," proclaimed Douglass, insisting that Americans must learn to accept this fact and to make the United States a home for people of all colors.

"We are here and here to stay," Douglass said of the black man's presence in America. "It is well for us and well for the American people to rest upon this as final."

On this note, Douglass's career came to a close. On February, 20, 1895, he attended a meeting in Washington of women's rights activists. Escorted to the speaker's platform by his old friend Susan B. Anthony, Douglass acknowledged the cheers of the crowd, who applauded his long devotion to the cause of women's rights. That night, while describing the day's events to his wife, Douglass was struck by a massive heart attack and died at the age of 77.

As news of Douglass's death spread throughout the country, crowds gathered at the Washington church where he lay in state to pay their respects. Black public schools closed for the day, and parents took their children for a last look at the famed leader. His wife and children accompanied his body back to Rochester, where he was laid to rest.

With Douglass's passing, a great era in black history came to an end. During his lifetime, he not only saw his people freed from their centuries of bondage, but helped them begin to live with whites as equal citizens in the United States. Although many of the rights and freedoms that blacks had won after the Civil War were taken away from them, Douglass advised his people not to despair:

> We still live, and while there is life there is hope. The fact that we have endured wrongs and hardships, which would have destroyed any other race . . . ought to strengthen our faith in ourselves and our future. Let us then . . . resolutely struggle on in the belief that there is a better day coming, and that we by patience, industry, uprightness, and economy may hasten that better day.

No one has struggled more resolutely for the rights of his people than Frederick Douglass. Born at a time when strong voices were desperately needed to cry out for freedom, he established himself as a powerful speaker for all men and women. ❧

CHRONOLOGY

February 1818	Born Frederick Bailey near Easton, Maryland.
1824	Works for Captain Aaron Anthony.
1826	Travels to Baltimore, Maryland to work for Hugh Auld.
March 1833	Returns to Anthony farm to work for Thomas Auld.
January 1834	Works for Edward Covey.
1835	Works for William Freeland.
1836	First escape plan fails; is imprisoned; sent back to Hugh Auld.
1837	Meets Anna Murray.
September 1838	Escapes to New York; sends for and marries Anna Murray; changes name to Frederick Douglass.
August 1841	Asked to speak at American Anti-Slavery Society meeting; invited to go on lecture tour.
May 1845	*Narrative of the Life of Frederick Douglass* is published; Douglass begins tour of England.
1847	Returns to the United States and begins lecture tour.
December 1847	Begins printing the *North Star.*
1848	Attends first women's rights convention.
1850	Becomes involved in the underground railroad after the passage of the Fugitive Slave Act.
1851	Breaks with William Garrison.
November 1859	Sails to England to begin lecture tour.
May 1860	Returns to the United States.
1863	Meets with President Abraham Lincoln to discuss the treatment of black soldiers during the Civil War.
1864	Meets with Lincoln to formulate plans to lead blacks out of the South in case of a Union defeat.
February 1866	Meets with President Andrew Johnson to discuss black suffrage.
July 1867	Declines Johnson's offer to head Freedman's Bureau.
March 1870	The Fifteenth Amendment is adopted and blacks are granted the right to vote; becomes editor of the *New National Era.*
1874	Becomes president of the Freedman's Savings and Trust Company.
1877	Becomes U.S. Marshal.
1880	Appointed recorder of deeds for Washington, D.C.
August 1882	Anna Douglass dies.
January 1884	Douglass marries Helen Pitts.
1889	Accepts post of American consul-general to Haiti.
1891	Resigns post and returns home.
February 20, 1895	Dies in Washington, D.C.

FURTHER READING

Douglass, Frederick. *Life and Times of Frederick Douglass.* New York: Collier Books, 1962.

————. *Narrative of the Life of Frederick Douglass: An American Slave.* Cambridge: Belknap Press of Harvard University, 1960.

Foner, Philip S. *The Life and Writings of Frederick Douglass: Early Years 1817–1849.* New York: International Publishers, 1950.

————. *The Life and Writings of Frederick Douglass: Pre–Civil War Decade 1850–1860.* New York: International Publishers, 1950.

————. *The Life and Writings of Frederick Douglass: The Civil War 1861–1865.* New York: International Publishers, 1952.

————. *The Life and Writings of Frederick Douglass: Reconstruction and After.* New York: International Publishers, 1955.

Huggins, Nathan Irvin. *Slave and Citizen: The Life of Frederick Douglass.* Boston: Little, Brown, 1980.

Quarles, Benjamin. *Frederick Douglass.* Washington, D.C.: The Associated Publishers, Inc., 1948.

INDEX

———————— •◐• ————————

PICTURE CREDITS

Anthony Family Papers, Dodge Collection, Maryland Hall of Records: p. 19; The Bettmann Archive: pp. 2, 3, 12, 13, 14, 16, 18, 21, 22, 24–25, 26, 28, 29, 31, 32, 33, 34, 36, 37, 38, 39, 40, 41, 42, 43, 44, 45, 46, 49, 50, 51, 52, 54, 55, 57, 58, 60, 61, 62, 63, 64, 65, 66, 67, 68, 69, 70, 72, 74, 75, 76, 77, 78, 79, 80, 81, 82, 83, 84, 86, 87, 88, 89, 90, 91, 92, 93, 94, 97, 98, 100, 101, 102, 104; Citadel Press: p. 23; *The Clarion Voice*, National Park Service: pp. 96, 103; Moorland-Spingarn Research Center, Howard University: p. 48; Courtesy of William B. Sears: p. 20; UPI/Bettmann News-photos: p. 10.

SHARMAN APT RUSSELL received her B.S. from the University of California at Berkeley and her M.F.A. from the University of Montana. She is the coauthor of *Built to Last: The Architectural History of Silver City, NM* and a feature writer for such magazines as *Darkroom Photography*, *National Gardening*, *New Mexico Magazine*, *New Mexico Wildlife*, and *Phoenix Home and Gardens*. At present, she teaches writing at Western New Mexico University and lives with her husband and children in the Mimbres Valley of southwestern New Mexico.

NATHAN IRVIN HUGGINS is W.E.B. Du Bois Professor of History and Director of the W.E.B. Du Bois Institute for Afro-American Research at Harvard University. He previously taught at Columbia University. Professor Huggins is the author of numerous books, including *Black Odyssey: The Afro-American Ordeal in Slavery*, *The Harlem Renaissance*, and *Slave and Citizen: The Life of Frederick Douglass*.